Endorsements

"Such a brilliant chap!

It's an excellent book by all standards."

**– Emmanuel Gyapong, Celebrated Banker,
Bank of America, USA**

"Terrific job. Kudos!"

– Rogers A. Stephen, CPA UK

"It's powerful!"

– Emmanuel Afriyie, News Anchor, Metro TV

"This book if diligently read has the potential to catapult
its reader from a life of little ambition to a "go-getter".
It's direct, on-point, relevant and most importantly very
practical in every aspect."

– Christiana Nana Yaa Acheampong,

CEO, Western Department Ltd.

Disclaimer

The author has taken reasonable precaution in preparing this book and believes that the facts presented in the book are accurate as of the date it is written. However, neither the publisher nor the author assumes responsibility for any errors or omissions. The author obtained the information contained in this book from sources he believes to be reliable: from his extensive reading, research, and his personal experiences, but particularly disclaim any liability ensuing the use or application of this book; and the information is not intended to serve as legal advice related to individual or corporate situations.

Published by:

ABN Communications Ltd

M: + (0) 233-509-36-36-07

Email: info@abnonline.org

Contact Author:

Email: ikadusei@abnonline.org

Dedication

This Book is dedicated to *Commence*, a social enterprise project of Africa Business Network (ABN) which is working to help achieve the United Nations Sustainable Development Goal

(SDG) 1: Zero Poverty by 2030

Acknowledgment

I owe a considerable depth of gratitude to many people across the four corners of the world who have in varied ways contributed to the coming out of this book. Special appreciation to my adorable wife, Mavis, my daughter Nhyiraba who continues to inspire me, my Dad Mr. Samuel Adusei and Mum Mrs. Gladys Adusei, my Godfather, Hon. Op. Abraham K. Adusei, all my siblings, relatives and wonderful team working in The ABN Organization. Special appreciation goes to Mr. Christopher Koramoah, Mr. Prince Adu-Afful, Mr. Emmanuel Gyapong, Ms. Christiana Nana Yaa Acheampong, Mr. Emmanuel Kwasi Afriyie and Ms. Rita Awuku for their immeasurable support in the coming out of this piece. Profound gratitude goes out to Mr. Rogers A. Stephen CPA, for avidly proofreading and editing this masterpiece of a book. To those supporting me and my projects behind the scene, I say God richly bless you. All glory be to God!

Hello Reader,

The greatest lie ever told by people - especially many below the ages of forty and fifty is that one day the goddess of good fortune will cross their path and suddenly everything they touch will turn into gold. Many people believe in this lie. They, therefore, continue to hold back, expectant of the day the goddess of good fortune will finally cross their path.

The greatest truth is that you are in control of your destiny. You can wait for one day to be successful or take today as day one, to become a man or woman of value.

This book, *How To Start Small* will set you on the path to success in business and in life. In the covers of this wonderful piece, I will reveal gripping real-life entrepreneurial stories, lessons and strategies underpinning world renowned globally competitive businesses.

Thank you!

J. K. Adusei
12th August, 2018
Ghana, West Africa

CONTENT   PG

CAUTION:

**CAREFULLY READ EVERY UNIT OF THIS
BOOK TO ACHIEVE MAXIMUM OUTCOME**

INTRODUCTION

I love to share my story. I love to share other people's stories too. This book stretches beyond any story I can ever tell. It is a solution. It is an answer to a conundrum – a real-life business challenge. Before you become judgemental of this book, its content and how it could be of value to you and your life situation, permit me to take a stride with you to reveal to you the life of the author of this book, How to Start Small, I.K Adusei.

Life is but an awful dream which you have to

wake up to correct. - **I.K Adusei**

I was born in the days when apartheid was brought to its knees. I didn't see the Berlin wall fall, neither did I see the end of the industrial age. I was just a few days old by then. I was born Ghanaian, and happily so. I am particularly happy to have been born Ghanaian not only for the rich political history, success and triumph of democracy, rule of law and capitalism, but rather for the abundance of opportunities which abound among a society of people far too reserved, laid back and comfortable with little or nothing.

January 29, 1989 was the year of my birth. I woke up from my 9 months nightmare into the arms of a local midwife with no formal training. My life may have been in danger, but thank God I survived my first hurdle.

My birthplace was in a remote bathroom in my father's house – a cute compound house he managed to put up for his family of eleven at Osiem – Akim, a town near Koforidua, Ghana's Eastern Regional capital. Amidst a myriad of church folks who lodged in our house full of joy and praise, the local midwife held me by the head and helped my mother to deliver a bouncy baby boy soon to be called Isaac Kwasi Adusei.

I cried as we all do on our first day on earth. With warm reception and excitement from my family and the church sojourners in our house, I saw the first day of my life, my first day on earth.

It is obvious you will come into this world crying, but try your best to leave with a smile on your face and that of those you leave behind.

Africa was celebrating the ruins of apartheid, and the world was in a transition from industrial age to information age. The World Wide Web was on the rise and the world had become a global village. Opportunities knew no boundaries and the world was but an even playing ground, everything in essence is possible in the information era.

Dreams are worth a leap of faith.

You may be cast down but never destroyed.

Born in such a rural community one could only expect me to have become at best a primary school or secondary school teacher since that was the best profession available at the time which most people could ever dream of.

Growing up was fun. As a promising child, as I learnt from home quite early in life, my immediate goal was to pursue the best in education. My parents were particularly more supportive of my education. I remember the first day my dad took me to school. It was the first preparatory school in town. I was as enthusiastic as I have always been about everything I love. My dad seemed more eager than I was as we walked several kilometres from our home to make my debut in a preparatory school located close to the cemetery. Life had already begun, and I was about four years old.

As far as school is concerned, I wasn't the brightest you could come across – though I was in most cases. I am more of a curious wide reader who at a very tender age took delight in reading encyclopaedias, atlases, autobiographies, biographies, etc. and books like Charles Dickens` David Copperfield, Adventures of Tom Sawyer, Oliver Twist, among other novels. I was very curious as a child and my teachers took particular delight in me.

Back home I was always punished for my uncooperative behaviour. Irrespective of my high academic laurels the spirit of stubbornness was always my guest. I was rowdy and very insolent as at age 10. My parents were very frustrated as it was seemingly impossible to control my incessant disobedience to laid down instructions.

Society makes the man. I agree strongly to this assertion. Society moulds the behaviour of individuals as one grows up.

Growing up in a Christian based society – as a child living in a church mission community, I happened to blend in quite well in terms of morals when growing up. By the time I got to Senior High School, specifically Prempeh College, Kumasi – Ghana, family, school and society had contributed tremendously to making me more disciplined, calm and purposeful. I was suddenly more disciplined, better dressed and more competitive in class not only academically but also in extracurricular activities including sports and leadership.

I became a responsible teenager as I transformed from my murky childhood. With the knowledge I had acquired from my wide reading, I learnt to be a better leader, public speaker and business enthusiast.

My father was more of a farmer than a public servant. As a retired Purchasing Clerk of Produce Buying Company (PBC), he is one of the most industrious in the East – Akim District of the Eastern Region. As a farmer, he worked hard in cultivating several acres of cocoa and teak which he owns till now.

I first learnt the ethics of hard work, sacrifice and commitment to life goals from my father. Through his hard work and that of my mum – who manned my father's licensed chemical store as well as taking care of the family, my father managed to send me and my other siblings and cousins through school. Most of us are now university graduates and others like me, well inspired to pursue higher learning.

In September 2008, I gained admission into University of Ghana, Legon to pursue a Bachelor of Arts Degree in Political Science, Psychology and Spanish. I had the option of dropping any of these courses in my second year and finish with a combined major in the two remaining courses or major and minor any of the courses in my final year. During my four years undergraduate training in Legon, I dropped Spanish in my second year, single majored Political Science and minored Psychology.

I was more informed of what I wanted from the university on my very first day at school. I wanted to establish a company and become my own boss. No wonder my days in school were characterized by running of my own student's organization which has metamorphosed into the company I am running today as CEO & Founder, The ABN Organization.
Learn more: www.abnonline.org.
The ABN Organization continues to venture into new businesses in areas of real estate, retail, media and commerce.

I am happily married to a wonderful and supportive woman Mavis and have been blessed with a lovely baby girl, Nhyiraba.

With my story most elaborately shared, I believe I can go ahead to share with you more stories and principles buried in the belly of my ground-breaking book, How to Start Small.

UNIT 1

HOW TO START SMALL

Are you a student?

● ● ● ● ●

"Your school may be there for decades or even centuries but your time there is limited."

I.K Adusei

Students have the best opportunity to become financially free. As you know, education is expensive but invaluable. Whoever doesn't assent to this truth will soon discover how expensive stupidity is.

Being a parent myself, I appreciate the enormity of the financial burden which education poses and above all the worth of an academic gift which I could hand down to my daughter. I am therefore very liberal and less conservative when it comes to spending on education (not limited to schooling), being it on myself or my family. My father, for instance, was not a 'rich rich' man but with his spending on education which reflects in the academic credentials and altitude his children have attained, people reckon him to be a very rich man.

My father spent a lot of money – hard earned money to put me and my siblings through school. My siblings and I enjoyed attending 'ivy league' schools in Ghana notably, Accra Academy, Prempeh College, Pope John Senior High School, Yaa Asantewaa Girls and so on. These schools are still top Senior High Schools in

Ghana. These facts, however, are less reflective of the main occupation of my father who is a farmer.

I know you have equally had the privilege of some education regardless of the size of your family's fortune. I know the answer is yes!

Let us now analyse the issue of starting a business having this rare insight into the cost of education at hand.

THE LIFEBLOOD OF BUSINESS IS MONEY

Any kind of legitimate money can start, grow and nurture a business.

Note here, the keyword is legitimate money. Only legitimate money can start and sustain your dream business. Illegitimate money will soon bring you to ruin.

People are more likely to financially support you if you are a student. Clichés like *youth are the future leaders* are still relevant today. Students enjoy a lot of sympathy from family, family friends, religious organizations,

society, donor agencies, the state and almost everyone in the world today.

See the number of scholarship schemes (free money) available to only students – not farmers, businessmen/women, drivers nor senior citizens. There is always some free money available for a student somewhere as long as that person continues to look for one.

HOW YOUR STUDENT ID CARD CAN HELP YOU START YOUR BUSINESS

Many students do not know what value their student identity (ID) cards hold. They only see it as a card which signifies their affiliation or membership of a certain educational institution. Many even see it as a pass to sitting or writing exams or sometimes (mostly among the boys) their ticket to getting more female friends in other educational institutions. There are some who even get a little feel of the value of their student's ID card when they present it at the gate of major events to either

be given a free pass or enjoy reduced (student) prices. Life is really kinder to students than school leavers.

So what is in a student ID card? As a business strategist and entrepreneur, I see an ID card as a ticket to enjoying access to free – legitimate multiple streams of income from businesses, individuals, state (s), donor agencies etc. These are streams of income which are natural, unrestrained and yet time-bound. These incomes will not run dry as long as you remain a student. Many people are able to access only a small proportion of this free money before they leave school. Yet, every student one way or the other enjoys a certain percentage of this free money. Those who are able to judiciously exhaust a large percentage of these streams of income are able to become successful entrepreneurs after leaving school without ever needing a 9 – 5 job in their lives. You can leave school with enough resources to create jobs rather than ending up as a job seeker. This is not your typical stream of income. You do not have control of the income sources. It is free and yet limited. Your ability to understand this (as you proceed further) and utilize this rich information will help you amass a fortune before you leave school.

THE VALUE OF THE STUDENT ID CARD

You are only a student for a short while. You will leave school sooner than you think. Your school may be there for decades or even centuries but your time there is limited.

In September 2008, I gained admission to study Political Science, Spanish and Psychology in University of Ghana. One of the very first Political Science lecturers who tutored me gave me a better appreciation of my status as a student. As one of the students in class that day, Dr. Evans Aggrey Darko one of my Political Science lecturers at the time asked a simple but intriguing question. He asked us to find out the meaning of the word *university*. A simple google search of the word university will give you a myriad of answers, yet no answer ever satisfied our curious lecturer, Aggrey Darko – as we affectionately called him.

Having failed to answer his question, Aggrey went back to the podium where he initially stood to lecture us on something I will never forget in life. In his own words, he defined a university as a *whole universe in one city*.

Everything you would like to do in life could be initiated in this city. Every race, religion, tribe, ethnicity could be found in this city. Nothing is ever impossible to accomplish in this city.

This broad yet focused definition of the word university had a telling effect on me from that day. It meant I had all the resources and network I needed to start achieving whichever dream I could dream of. The sky was even not the limit. My ID card was a 4-year VISA for me to kick start my dreams and make it come true. I was in a city in which the universe as we know it is situated. My ID card had more value than I ever taught it had.

This definition dispelled the common notion which most students hold that, *"when I complete school I would like to be..."* In the university (like any other level of education) you can start becoming whoever you want to be. Simply put, you can be whoever you want to be while you are in school. Start, whichever way possible, to be who you want to be before you leave school. Your future self depends on what you do with your time in school.

YOUR SCHOOL ID CARD IS YOUR FIRST BUSINESS CARD

To start small in the area of a business venture, don't belittle yourself as a student. Your school ID carries more value in all aspects of your business life including access to capital, finance, media publicity, market, marketing etc.

HOW TO USE YOUR STUDENT ID CARD TO RAISE CAPITAL

HOW TO RAISE CAPITAL FROM FAMILY

Parents supply your first stream of income – your 'chop money'. Know that part of your pocket money will soon become your *business money*. But mind you, your business money is not part of your pocket money.

You can save part of your small pocket money as initial capital to start your business. Accept this fact, if you can't save money, you can't start a business. Money makes business (the world) go round.

My first business capital was a GHC 5.00 savings from my monthly pocket money of GHC 100.00 which I received from home every month. I soon opened an investment account with a *good* bank with GHC 50.00. Some good banks have students' accounts. These accounts can take initial deposits of as low as GHC 10.00.

Students often attract the sympathy of their siblings, uncles, aunties, family friends, neighbours and other distant relations and acquaintances. These sympathies result in windfall capital (monies which are usually unexpected) for your business venture. Students with no business objectives often squander such monies on profligate and frivolous expenditures soon to be going cap – in – hand to these same benefactors for financial assistance or in other cases for help to secure jobs after school. The respect and judicious use of such monies when you are in school will remain a trusted basis for your financial freedom in the immediate future.

HOW TO RAISE CAPITAL FROM RELIGIOUS ORGANIZATIONS

Churches, mosques, Hindu temples and traditionalist societies, etc are replete with people who are very supportive and generous. Giving is an act which comes from the heart. Nonetheless, be careful and always question the motive behind the giving of strange gifts especially from friends, acquaintances or strangers.

Jesus said, let the children come to me for theirs is the kingdom of God. Students and young people are good targets for alms giving or financial support. Students are supported by religious bodies mostly to project them as trail-blazers for the up and coming. This presents an enormous opportunity for students (youth) to gain financial and other assistance in their chosen entrepreneurial venture.

Events like book launch, album launch, product launch and sampling etc could be conducted by students in churches to generate capital for their business start-ups.

You cannot imagine how much financial support you can garner in the church using the student (future leader) trump card.

Whenever I have the opportunity to speak to student groups and associations I usually share with them the *joy of being a student congregant.* Pastors take a peculiar delight in introducing their student congregants (mostly university students) to the rest of the congregation.

For example, if a pastor is introducing a student congregant from University of Ghana, he will usually say, "Let's welcome back from school Randolph Arthur a first-year Computer Engineering student of University of Ghana, Legon." This type of introduction will usually be followed by an incessant round of applauds. Wouldn't it? Of course!

No one seems to quantify the amount of favour and good fortune available for students when their ID cards are still active and not expired. In the presence of creativity, industry and common sense, students can actively harvest this rare favour and mutual support from their church folks to serve as capital for their businesses even before their ID cards ever expire.

Now, imagine the kind of response which will ensue when Randolph completes university and after a year or two his pastor decides to introduce him to the same congregation. A typical introduction would be, "Here is Randolph Arthur who completed University of Ghana three years ago."

Now, are you sure Randolph will receive the same applauds he received when he was introduced as a student? I'm not sure. I doubt he will even receive 1% or even any applauds at all. The usual reaction would be, "Ok cool. So what is he doing now?" The ID card has expired and his favour, unfortunately, expired with it.

HOW TO ATTRACT CORPORATE SUPPORT AS A STUDENT

The youth card is a healthy trump card used to attract support from the corporate world. Youth brands usually enjoy endorsement from the corporate world especially the not – for – profit youth-led businesses. In Ghana, youth-led companies like Farmer Line, Tech Era, Women in Vogue, etc were all started by young Ghanaians below the ages of 24 years, nurturing their businesses from school. These youth-led businesses have enjoyed numerous grants, exposure and financial support from local and international corporate institutions and donor agencies. With the right business model and exposure, the student (youth) trump card has the potential of providing a healthy milieu to attract corporate support for youth-led businesses.

As an undergraduate student at University of Ghana, I nurtured my entrepreneurial skills through the successful setting up of a student organization on campus. As a broke level 200 student in school, I was able to organize a three day Pan-African Leadership Conference with participants attending the event from several African countries including Nigeria and Liberia. The main conference was held at Africa Regent Hotel, a four-star hotel in Accra.

My business model at the time was to heavily rely on my leadership and negotiation skills to rally a team of inexperienced yet effective student event organizers to help me put together such a wonderful conference – as it turned out to be. The event was heavily supported by the media and a number of corporate bodies who saw in my team, a strong-willed student group who had the potential to change the world. The student ID card was in massive use and the success of the well - attended and fruitful conference was born out of the divine favour of God and the tag that others placed on us as ambitious students at the time.

Now the lesson here is, it is possible for a student from a humble background to organize high - level international events with little or no money using the privileges that come with holding a valid students ID card.

HOW TO USE MEDIA PUBLICITY TO GATHER CHEAP CAPITAL

Research shows that the world population is largely youthful. In our part of the world, Africa, we have the fastest – growing and most youthful population in the world – making up over 40% under the ages of 15 and 20% between the ages of 15 – 24 according to a survey by Africa Development Bank (AfDB) conducted in 2017.

The youth all over the world constitute the largest chunk of the voting populace and thus demand a lot from their respective governments in terms of participation in governance, demand for employment, social inclusion and protection etc. The media acts mostly as the fourth arm of government in most advanced and fledgling democracies. The media has become a conduit through which the government hears the sentiments of the youth.

Post World War II media agencies have become apparently a pro-youth media which continues to shape events in the 21st century towards the achievement of what I call 'youth power'. Today, the media is at the forefront of driving youth leadership and entrepreneurship agenda.

In Ghana, the youth enjoy free or highly subsidized opportunities to sell their ideas or promote their start-up businesses and non-profits throughout the print and electronic media. Now more than ever, it is easier for any youth to approach or be approached by a media house to talk about their cause or start-up business as a way of projecting role models for society as well as attracting the engagement, commitment and listenership of the youth who largely dominate society.

Whether you see this happening or not, it is a reality which doesn't need to be overemphasized. You have a chance to use this reality to promote your idea, cause or small business without spending as the 'big boys' do. Approach a media house with your requests or proposals if you doubt what you are reading – this is a gold nugget handed out to you for free.

HOW TO USE SOCIAL MEDIA TO RAISE CAPITAL

A joke that has gone viral on social media posits:

"I got the job."

➤ 264 Likes, 74 Comments

"I started my own business."

➤ 7 Likes, 3 Comments

People are often ready to celebrate when you find a job, but become indifferent when you tell them you are starting your own business.

This situation is largely born out of the perception that *entrepreneurship* is *a lonely road less travelled by*. It is true though! Entrepreneurship is a hard bumpy road less travelled by.

However, some social media platforms like crowdfunding platforms which include, GoFundMe, Indiegogo, Kickstarter, generosity.com etc. are more supportive of entrepreneurial ventures.

These crowdfunding sites make it easier to win financial support from around the world to fund your business venture or non-profit cause. You do this by creating and sharing your start-up story on any of these crowdfunding platforms to be able to raise money to kick start, continue or complete your entrepreneurial project.

On these platforms, you only have to be creative enough to craft a campaign message which has the potential of attracting financial support in the form of donations from known and unknown donors around the world.

Many of such well-crafted campaigns have resulted in students and youth-led businesses raising a lot of money to fund their enterprises. This approach will be further discussed as we move forward.

UNIT 2

HOW TO START SMALL

Are you a fresh graduate?

• • • • •

"To be able to find a job, raise capital and exit a

company tomorrow to start your own, you need to have

safe and secure entry and exit strategy."

I.K Adusei

The most common thing most parents request of their wards is *to go to school, get a safe secure job with benefits and live happily ever after.*

Most graduates in Ghana after their one-year national service will often love to be 'maintained' in their respective places of work often with little success. Most graduates today remain unemployed after school for a long time sometimes spanning beyond 10 years.

Graduates who want to start their own businesses after school can consider saving part of their national service allowance as seed capital for their start-up businesses. They can similarly use their already established working environment to study and understand what works and what doesn't work in the corporate space.

All in all, national service personnel must consider their one-year national service as a time to put some life in their own entrepreneurial ventures through shrewd spending, saving and investment.

As a national service person in Cape Coast posted to the National Road Safety Commission, I accepted my posting with joy and enthusiasm as I saw the opportunity to learn from a new working environment.

I had at that time not been to Cape Coast before. I foresaw the unique prospect to experience life outside my comfort zone. Prior to my posting, I had managed to secure myself a national service placement at the AU Diaspora African Forum (AU DAF) office in Cantonments – Accra. I leveraged on my excellent working relationship with the President of AU DAF, H.E Dr. Erieka Bennett who participated in one of the Pan-African Conferences I organized while in school.

However, after I sighted my original posting by the National Service Secretariat (NSS) to serve at the Road Safety Commission's Regional Office in Cape Coast, I sought permission from H.E Bennett to accept the posting from the NSS. This may look like an ill-informed decision, so to speak. I understand. On the contrary, it was a great decision I took. H.E Bennett respected my position and was pleased to welcome me to her outfit whenever I deemed it fit. I believe she saw in me a highly spirited entrepreneurial-minded young man who had a taste for adventure and the pursuit of purpose.

I enjoyed my time in Cape Coast anyway. I saved and invested money to build a financial nest for the successful publishing of my first book, From Nowhere to Somewhere. As it turned out, my first book was in itself a precursor to making more money to invest in my numerous business interests.

I managed to create strategic business networks and connections during my time at the Road Safety Commission in Cape Coast. These contacts were made through my participation in conferences and numerous road safety outreach and sensitization programs we embarked on. Most of these contacts have been crucial to my seeming business success today.

ENTREPRENEURIAL CHOICES

As a graduate entrepreneur, you are on your own. You should know that you hold the steering wheel in your quest for success. You are, however, not a loner in this journey of life. There is a wide network of entrepreneurs globally taking the same journey with you.

In another breath, you can find a day time job and nurture your small business on the side or like me take the entrepreneurial leap of faith steering your ship against the tides of life towards your desired destination.

There are others who harbour the ambition of finding a job to help raise capital and experience and later exit to start their own businesses. All these options are widely available for you to be able to start small and win big in business and in life. All these options, nonetheless, come with their respective pros and cons.

1. FIND A DAY TIME JOB AND MIND YOUR OWN BUSINESS ON THE SIDE

Life after school is no joke. It is a trying moment for a lot of people especially those with limited corporate network. Graduates who find themselves wanting after school in the areas of job search mostly lacked what is called *school - work balance*.

They failed to know that university is nothing short of a whole universe in one city. There were more social and corporate networks available in those universities they had their degrees from. Most of their potential employers participated in events and conferences which took place in their respective universities and those on other campuses.

Most of their potential employers had spaces in their offices for interns which has the potential of culminating in future employment if interns prove themselves resourceful over time.

Finding a day time job and minding your own business on the side could help in the creation of jobs. This is, however, not a simple thing to do. Mind you, if it were simple everyone would be doing it.

A safe secure job with benefits alone is a free ticket to living a financially stressful life. Living from paycheque to paycheque is a real nightmare for most working adults since their take-home pay barely takes them home.

Finding a day time job can help you raise capital. This could be done through careful spending, saving and investment in order to raise the needed capital to set up and operate your own business.

MIND YOUR OWN BUSINESS

To be able to raise more capital to fund your business pursuit, the first business you set up should not necessarily be your *main business*. Your first business could be petty trading in consumable items varying from clothing, food items, electronic gadgets etc. You can carry out your petty trading at church (or your place of worship), workplace or in front of your house.

There is no real business school like a business you set up yourself. With your own business, you can learn quickly about what works and what doesn't work, as you do your utmost to manage your cash flow.

Cash flow is simply money that comes into your business from the sale of products or provision of services. It is also money that goes out of your business in the form of expenditure or expenses. Efficient management of cash flow in any business will ensure its rapid growth.

A business has positive cash flow when it uses its money prudently to make more profit. Negative cash flow is attributed to lack of proper financial management in a business which results in financial loss.

For example, let's assume you run a booming T-Shirt retail business. Averagely, you make daily sales of GHC 300. And out of your daily sales of GHC 300, you make the following daily expenses: GHC 100 on nightlife and GHC 100 as housekeeping expenses each day.

These bad liquidity practices in your business (thus, making expenditures which do not generate profits for your business) amount to negative cash flow.

If your business is run in this manner, you will soon have to fall on external funding to support your operations no matter how much cash or inventory (stock) your business has.

On the other hand, if you calculate your profits each day, and for instance, you invest your profits wisely in your sales strategy in order to induce more sales resulting in more profits, your business will be making positive cash flow which will result in business growth.

So you can actually transfer your savings from your day time job into setting up and growing your own business on the side.

Your small business venture can generate more profits than a huge car rental company. It is not the size of a business that makes it profitable but the efficient management of cash flow.

The ensuing chapters will shed more light on cash flow and cash flow management as well as provide more insight into how you can set up an efficient and profitable enterprise.

2. STARTING A CAPITAL INTENSIVE BUSINESS

AS A YOUNG GRADUATE

Most people love to start big businesses or enter capital intensive business ventures from the start. So they choose to find a good job to raise enough capital and experience.

It is tough to start capital intensive businesses. It makes a lot of sense to brace yourself up financially before you launch yourself into such a business. Capital intensive businesses may also require high corporate network and managerial skills to be profitable. Finding a job to raise capital and skill here is a worthwhile activity.

For example, setting up an auto parts manufacturing company, an airline company, a university, etc. requires a lot of start-up capital and know-how. One may need to save and invest for a long time to be able to start such business ventures.

The nature of the business also requires a robust and resolute business model coupled with an excellent market survey. Any trial and error here will result in dire financial consequences.

Graduates who want to succeed in this area, can find a job in the area of their interest, learn on the job and attain the needed skill and capital before they go-all-out on their own.

The problem arises often when graduates with the desire to establish capital intensive businesses find jobs in sectors unrelated to their field of interest.

This type of dream more often than not becomes a pipe dream. The challenge is not that of capital alone. Capital intensive businesses require a high level of know-how and give less room for trial and error. Any technical glitch in the initial stages can result in the owners landing themselves in a dire financial mess which could take years or forever to overcome.

AVOID THE RAT RACE

Another challenge is the ability to have a resolute entry and exit strategy. To be able to find a job, raise capital and exit a company tomorrow to start your own, you need to have a safe and secure entry and exit strategy. With this, I mean you start by having the end in mind.

Failure to carefully plan one's entry and exit strategy will cause workers to fall in the *9 am -5 pm trap* which most working adults find themselves in. This is a stressful lifestyle associated with working long hours just to make ends meet.

The struggle from paycheque to paycheque leaves unsuspecting workers with little or no money to invest in their dreams. It is an uncanny roller-coaster ride which makes one a perfect fit in someone else's business at the expense of the freedom that comes with running your own business. Many unfortunate people without an entry and exit strategy break their back all day long to help other people accomplish their dreams at the expense of their own health and financial freedom. This is what we term in the corporate circles as the *rat race*. Most unhappy working adults find themselves in this tight yet inevitable situation. Don't be one of them.

THE PATRICK AWUAH STORY

Dr. Patrick Awuah, Founder of Ashesi had an exit strategy when he applied for a high paying job with the Silicon Valley Company, Microsoft. As an ambitious young man, he managed to enter Swarthmore College with a full scholarship from Ghana.

After his undergraduate studies at Swarthmore College in the USA where he graduated with a bachelor's degree in Engineering and Economics, young Patrick landed a high paying job at Microsoft.

From 1989-1997, Dr. Patrick Awuah worked with Microsoft as a Software Engineer and Programs Manager. There he spearheaded the development of the dial-up internetworking technologies. He was widely praised for his exceptional ability to solve major hydra-headed engineering problems during his time there.

As an employee of Microsoft, Patrick had the dream of establishing an institution of higher learning in the areas

of Science, Technology, Engineering and Mathematics (STEM) among other academic disciplines in Africa. The vision was to set up a citadel of learning in Africa that will provide world-class academic tuition comparable to Ivy League Colleges in the USA to raise the next generation of contemporary African leaders.

As part of his exit strategy, Patrick quit his job at Microsoft in 1997 and enrolled in UC Berkeley's Hass

School of Business the same year to focus his attention on building a business plan for Ashesi. At school, he travelled to Ghana with some of his colleague graduate students to conduct a feasibility study on the prospects of setting up a private university in Ghana.

After graduating in 1999, he moved back to Ghana with his wife Rebecca Awuah, a Software Testing Engineer who Patrick met at Microsoft. They later became the Founders of Ashesi University.

Finding a job to raise capital to set up a capital intensive business requires a robust entry and exit plan. Only a tactical few will succeed with this approach.

3. TAKING A LEAP OF FAITH

Entrepreneurship is a beautiful ride. It is one which is not recommended for chicken-hearted souls. Taking a leap of faith can get you started. This, however, does not mean embarking on Formula One race without appropriate protective gear. Instead, it calls for readiness for the long haul, regardless of what dangers one might potentially face.

To take a leap of faith you must expect the best and as well be prepared for the worst. Fortune has always favoured the brave.

There are many entrepreneurial lessons one could have learnt before graduating from school. These lessons include financial discipline, prudent saving and investments to start a business, sales and marketing skills, internships (of purpose) without pay, leadership skills development etc. These skills are the anchor used to weather the turbulent storms which entrepreneurship presents.

Putting on the armour of core entrepreneurial skills is the sure way to withstand the many challenges which present themselves as one decides to become an entrepreneur right from school. Prior preparation surely improves the chances of survival.

When you take a leap of faith you are usually confronted with the challenge of raising quick capital to secure all the needed resources and inputs to start a business. This challenge may or may not take a long time to overcome. Your ability to overcome such challenges largely depends on how prepared you are for the entrepreneurial journey.

In taking a leap of faith, chances of success are not guaranteed. However, those who succeed, sooner than later become celebrated business magnates.

Taking a leap of faith with prior preparation is my best recommendation to young graduates who want to be millionaires or pursue financial independence.

Let me share with you a story from the entrepreneurial pursuit of Aliko Dangote.

THE DANGOTE STORY

Aliko Dangote is a Nigerian business magnate, investor, and owner of the Dangote Group with interests in commodities in Nigeria, other African countries and currently in Nepal, Asia. As a primary school boy, Dangote recounts an incidence where he bought and sold cartons of candy to his colleagues and neighbours just to make money. When he graduated from Al-Azar University in Cairo, Egypt, in 1977 at the age of 21, Dangote took a loan of USD $3,000 (which he repaid within three months of business) from his uncle Sani Dangote to set up his first business in the Dangote Group.

Dangote after school took a leap of faith to embark on his entrepreneurial journey. His strides in his early entrepreneurial success were never without the entrepreneurial skills he had learnt in his formative years from his maternal grandfather Sanusi Dantata – one of the richest merchants to have ever come from Kano. The business connections and the network he made along the way coupled with the rich counsel he took from mentors like his uncle Sani Dangote who loaned him his initial start-up capital of USD $3,000 led to his success.

Very few Africans from privileged backgrounds are as successful as Aliko Dangote who according to Forbes

Magazine is currently having a net worth of USD$ 14.1 billion making him the undisputed richest black man in the world.

Dangote's switch from commodity trading, comprising sugar, flour, rice, cement etc., to the manufacturing of same in 1997 holds the key to his corporate dominance and success.

Many will argue that Dangote's privileged family background accounts for his current financial success, but not too many privileged kids ever become the wealthiest business magnates in their generation. A lot happens when you have the guts to dream big and take a leap of faith. Don't limit yourself!

UNIT 3

HOW TO START SMALL

Are you a business owner?

• • • • •

"Every global business first started in a local setting."

I.K Adusei

―――――――――――――――――――――――――――――

A business owner reading this book may either be having some cash flow challenges or wanting new ways to build a long term globally competitive business.

In either case, this book is for you.

This section will address the cardinal pillars for the growth of any globally oriented local business.

Every global business first started in a local setting. However, most local businesses either fail at birth or continue to remain localized and struggling. There are many cardinal principles which you can follow in your bid to start small and grow big.

This article by Strive Masiyiwa, the richest man in Zimbabwe and the Group President of Econet Wireless has some of the fundamental principles I would like to share with you in this book. This is how he puts it in his simple and well-crafted article I chanced on.

"THE BIGGEST SECRETS FOR TURNING YOUR SMALL BUSINESS INTO A BIG BUSINESS PART 1

Your business must have a life separate from you!

Years ago I shared with you the story of an old man who had a supermarket at a popular location. He boasted that he started his day at 4 am and left at 12 am.

His business never grew because two of the Ps were missing:

- ❖ **People:** He did not hire people with management and leadership skills to run his business.
- ❖ **Process:** He did not invest in the processes that would have allowed him to run multiple locations with lots of time to spare.

You don't ever need to visit a business if these two Ps are in place!

When your business is small, you obviously must work every day and every night to make it a success, with energy and passion, and with a deep desire to make it bigger. Now I know some of you are working towards a future where your business grows from a small business to a big one. Keep at it, because no matter how small your business is right now, what I am going to say applies to you, too.

The three Ps are:

- ❖ People
- ❖ Product

❖ Process

If you are dreaming of building a business that grows very big, I want to give you another perspective and share a few important secrets on this same topic.

Let's talk.

You have heard the expression "get a life"?

Your business also has a life!

It's important to allow your business "to get a life of its own," separate from you. It must be separate from you. It must be a separate living persona that has its own needs, separate from yours. You are not the business and the business is not you.

Imagine you run a cash business like a supermarket and a dear relative comes in with an emergency asking for money. Can you say to that person, "I'm sorry I have no money, what I have belongs to the business"?

People who run big businesses never treat the money of the business as their own. If this surprises you, then you are not yet ready for the big league!

A friend came to me once and asked me to lend him some money and I said I didn't have any. I could see the bitterness in his face as he said, "Everyone knows you have money because your businesses are doing well."

"The business is really doing well, but I'm not the business," I replied. "The two are different from each other."

Now if you're new to big business, you will not accept this, but if you went to Bill Gates or Patrice Mostsepe they will tell you the same.

Let me tell you, if you cannot do that, you will never be able to own a truly big business.

Tough talk? You better believe it!

Similarly, you cannot take the money belonging to the business to build a house for your family or buy a new car.

You are only entitled to your salary which should be fixed and taken only when others get paid. You are also entitled to a small portion of the profit, taken only from year 4 of successive years of profit. Cap it at 25%.

I have known some absolutely brilliant, innovative entrepreneurs in Africa and yet they struggled with this one thing. They would not allow a business to have a separate life from theirs.

The entrepreneur who allows the business to have its own life is the one who builds a big business."

My take: Research has shown that 90% of small businesses fail in the first 5 years of inception. 9 out of 10 in the remaining 10% of the businesses that survive the first five years, go on to fail in the ensuing 5 years.

The business world is a turbulent place. It punishes the ill-informed and ill-prepared business owners and rewards those who keep learning, innovating and improving their entrepreneurial skills as they carry out their day-to-day activities.

It, therefore, behoves on small business owners to develop the right entrepreneurial mindset which is needed to create successful and globally competitive businesses. Take a quick break and reflect on Strive Masiyiwa's revolutionary article on "The Biggest Secrets for Turning Your Small Business Into a Big Business."

In Unit 12, you will be presented with the checklist for starting a business and succeeding in style.

UNIT 4

HOW TO START SMALL

Are you an employee?

• • • • •

"The grass is always greener on the other side of fear.

Taking an entrepreneurial leap of faith is no mean task.
The brave often succeed, leaving behind the masses

who are chicken-hearted."

I.K Adusei

Getting a *good* job today calls for a massive celebration. A good job is defined by many as one which is *high paying* with excellent benefits. Some of these high paying jobs do a lot to guarantee job security as long as employees remain loyal to such businesses, institutions or firms. Government workers; military, paramilitary, police officers, public health workers, teachers and so on usually enjoy job security as part of their terms of employment which requires a life-long service.

People are pleased to have job security. Ironically, the word JOB is the acronym for JUST OVER BROKE or JOURNEY OF BORROWERS. Alarming as it sounds, employees for centuries have never been satisfied with their paycheque. Employees' demand for job security is at sharp variance with business owners' demand for financial security.

While employees work hard for job security, business owners provide job security in exchange for their own financial security.

Employees, therefore, need to break free from their over-reliance on their monthly paycheque which barely takes them home.

Employees can shift the goal post to attract other streams of income in order to ensure financial sustainability in their daily lives.

Similarly, employees can take a jump from employee to full-time business owners. Jumping from employee to business owner requires a far-sighted exit strategy. This will help mitigate the shocks which come along with starting a business. There is definitely going to be a situational shift when one decides to take a jump from employee to owner. There should be enough preparation in order to have a perfect transition.

HOW TO CREATE MULTIPLE

STREAMS OF INCOME

Robert T. Kiyosaki in his classic book, Rich Dad Poor Dad which has sold millions of copies worldwide shares this advice about how employees can create multiple streams of income. He said, by taking care of their day time jobs and minding their own businesses on the side, employees can succeed in the realm of entrepreneurship.

Creating multiple streams of income is the key to financial freedom. Many are desirous of financial freedom but few are ready to commit to the principles that undergird the realization of same.

You can't keep doing the same thing over and over again and expect different results. Wealth creation has its own formula. This is the same with poverty. To move from financial distress to financial security, there are some financial principles one must master.

FINANCIAL PRINCIPLES ON MULTIPLE STREAMS OF INCOME

I. Financial Discipline

Financial discipline is the anchor of financial freedom. The most financially successful people in the world more often than not, are financially disciplined individuals. Financial discipline is the ability to withhold present financial gratifications for future financial gains. To create wealth you should be able to forgo the immediate pleasures of the middle-class life which is mainly characterized by expenditure on luxury goods, expensive clothing, food and frolicsome belongings which they acquire with monies they don't even have just to impress their neighbours and friends. Rather than focusing on building their asset portfolios first, people with low financial discipline spend to keep up with the Joneses.

"The plans of the diligent lead to profit as surely as haste leads to poverty."
- Proverbs 21:5

To be financially disciplined:

1. Spend prudently

Wealth creation requires diligence. Many are those who desire to count their chicks before they are hatched. To be able to create a surplus, you need to spend prudently. Prudent spending requires you to take care of the pennies and allow the pounds to take care of itself.

In today's world, the average workers' take-home pay does not take him or her far. It is therefore difficult to survive in a month without borrowing, left alone save.

Many therefore end the month with a mountain of debt heaped up for the subsequent month. Deep within this mountain of debt are expenses on so-called discounted goods which end up in litter bins and storerooms.

Prudent spending will create a surplus which could be invested in your new business idea.

2. Don't spend on consumables spend on production

All the goods and services you pay for on a daily basis are created by individuals like you who have effectively positioned themselves to monetize their ideas and make money from the many problems plaguing our society.

To create multiple streams of income, you need to think of creative ways to solve problems around you in order to make a profit. By so doing you will be shifting your mind from the mentality of consumption to that of production.

To become financially independent you need to save enough money from your daily expenditure in order to create surplus which could be invested in your new business with the aim of creating new products or services.

Wealth creation requires a higher degree of creativity.

Whenever you go to the malls, do endeavour to look out for shelf spaces for your own products. Don't only go shopping for your favourite brands.

3. Know the difference between assets and liabilities. One of the single most important rules for wealth creation I have ever learnt is this: *Know the difference between assets and liabilities and choose to buy assets.*

Assets are simply the things you own that pay you. In Robert Kiyosaki's book Rich Dad Poor Dad, he made the argument that your house is not an asset. It is a liability.

According to him, if the purpose of owning a house is just to live in with your family, then your house is simply a liability, not an asset. Your house doesn't pay you at the end of the month, rather, it takes money away from you in the form of property taxes, maintenance and repairs, landscaping, electricity, water and gas bills etc.

This same house could however, be an asset under a different circumstance. For example, providing a boys' quarters on your property for rental purposes.

In this case, your bills and property taxes could be paid for at the end of the month by your tenants living in your boys' quarters.

In such a situation, your house or property becomes an asset since it pays you at the end of the month.

Similarly, if you put up adjoining shops, semi-detached apartments or office spaces in your house for business or offer them for rent, you will be making your house an asset since that will create for you multiple streams of income.

Liabilities are basically the things you own that cost you money. These things may be your house, cars, household appliances like TV, washing machines, gas/electric oven, furniture etc.

When you decide to spend your money buying more assets, your assets will soon take care of all your liabilities and make you financially independent and wealthy. If you keep buying liabilities – things you own that cost you money, you will soon be consumed by debt.

4. Learn to multiply your seeds

There is a parable in the bible which talks about a master who upon embarking on a journey decided to hand out talents to his servants.

He gave the first servant five talents. The second, three talents and the third, one.

Upon his return, the good master realized that the first servant had multiplied his talents by two folds and therefore had ten talents. The second had done the same and had six talents. However, the last servant hid his talent under a stone and had only a single talent to show.

When the master had realized what the last servant had done, in Matthew 25:26-29 (NIV), "The master replied, you wicked and lazy servant! So you knew that I harvest where I have not sown and gather where I have not scattered seed? Well then, you should have put the money on deposit with the bankers, so that when I returned I would have received it back with interest. Take the talent from him and give it to the one who has ten talents. For everyone who has will be given more and he will have abundance."

This principle of multiplying seeds in itself predates the Bible. Consider it as one of God's blessings to humankind – a promise of abundance to whoever is diligent at multiplying his or her talents.

5. Know that as an entrepreneur you only have yourself to impress.

Entrepreneurship is not a popularity contest. It is not an arena for the display of wealth, neither a competition for who is who in the world of business. It is far from it.

Jeff Bezos is the richest individual in the world today. His real-time net worth as I write today stands at USD $ 163.3 billion, checking from Forbes real-time rankings. As of June 2018, his net worth was USD $112 billion, checking from the same source. His closest ally Bill Gates has a real-time net worth of USD $ 95 billion.

It is likely you may not have heard of this till now. Jeff Bezos is the Founder of the e-commerce leviathan, Amazon. He foundered Amazon from his garage in Seattle, USA on July 5, 1994.

Over the years Amazon has been engaged in a massive recapitalization exercise mainly using retained earnings from the company. This means that the company keeps reinvesting its profits to create more positive cash flow and develop its systems. Until recently, shareholders of

Amazon had not received dividends for years throughout the recapitalization exercise.

Jeff Bezos was missing out from Forbes list of top 5 richest men in the world for several decades till the year 2016 and 2017.

In 2018 he emerged as Forbes Richest Man overthrowing Bill Gates whose net worth stood at USD$ 90 billion as at June 2018. Jeff Bezos is the first person ever to exceed the net worth of USD$ 150 billion in the 3 decades of Forbes operations.

Keep a low profile just to be able to increase your assets and create more positive cash flow. Many people who are expectant of you keeping up with the Joneses will decide to ridicule you but always bear in mind that, entrepreneurship is not a popularity contest. You have but yourself alone to impress. Keep this in mind and go for gold. There is no time to impress people whose predisposition have always been that of hatred and envy. The world is yours if you are able to do this! Go out there and make yourself proud.

II. Cash Flow Management

The second financial principle of creating multiple streams of income is cash flow management.

Cash flow refers to money that comes into and goes out of your business. Among other salient factors, it is the resourceful management of cash flow, thus income and expense in any business that makes the business succeed or fail. Proper cash flow management will lead to more profits and thus business expansion. Poor liquidity practices will result in debt and poor performance of any business.

At the utmost, businesses must try as much as possible to reduce their costs/expenses and increase their income/revenue.

Whenever you find a business struggling, the crust of the failure will be akin to the poor management of the business' cash flow.

Top 4 Ways on how to manage cash flow:

1. Your business money is not your money.

Your *business money* is your business money. This is a hard and fast rule for business success. Many people invest their monies in business ventures only to be dependent on the business capital for their survival.

Most table top businesses are conducted in this manner. Business owners who frequently dip their hands in and out of their business accounts, either to spend their projected income or deplete their capital will soon come to learn that, they did not have a business in the first place.

As a small business owner, you have to pay yourself a specific salary each month which should be paid after all your other expenditures are paid for. Any attempt to mistaken your business money for your personal money will be a precursor to your looming obliteration as an entrepreneur.

2. Your business must have a life of its own.

Money is the lifeblood of business. To make efficient use of the cash flow in your business, you need to keep your business capital intact (untouched).

Set a threshold for your cash outflow (expenditure) in order not to spend your business capital. This will keep your business commercially viable to help maximize your profits at the end of the day.

Mind you, your business has to pay for its own expenditure whether your sales are high or low. These expenditures include rent, office supply, restocking inventory, utility bills, staff salaries etc.

At all times in your business life, you should bear in mind that *cash is king*! Keeping a considerable amount of cash in your business over and above your operating capital will keep your business afloat in turbulent times.

3. Protect your purse.

When I began to diversify the services of The ABN Organization, I opened a new office location for trade and commerce. From the start, I encountered a common but deadly financial loss which could have easily been avoided.

I hired the services of a very good painter who did a great job painting my office location. After he was done painting, I discussed with him my intention to tile the floor and asked whether he knew a good tiler who would give me a fair price.

The problem arose when the painter managed to convince me that he was an expert in laying rubber tiles – a cheaper but quality option for the decoration of my floor. Being a good friend, I believed him and gave him the contract to get the job done. In the end, I lost my money after having trusted a painter with my money and conscience to deliver a good tiling job. The whole floor was messed up with rubber tiles which couldn't stick on the floor. I later got a proper tiler to remove and fix the mess and replace it with ceramic tiles.

This situation played back to me while I flipped through the pages of the book, *The Richest Man in Babylon* by George S. Clason a year later. In his book, he gave a piece of similar advice on protecting the purse.

After Arkad (who became the richest man in Babylon) had committed a similar mistake of trusting a brick maker with his money to undertake a joint jewel business, Algamish (his mentor) muttered, "Every fool must learn,' he growled, 'but why trust the knowledge of a brick maker about jewels? Would you go to the bread maker to inquire about the stars? No, by my tunic, you would go to the astrologer, if you had power to think. Your savings are gone, youth, you have jerked your wealth-tree up by the roots. But plant another. Try again, and next time if you would have advice about jewels, go to the jewel merchant. If you would know the truth about sheep, go to the herdsman."

4. Identify ways to create more positive cash flow.

You need to find creative ways to invest your profits to create more positive cash flow. You need to study your business critically to identify the areas that need investment to make more profit. Your sales team may need to be retrained to sharpen their skills. Your security systems may need to be upgraded to curb the incidence of burglary, shoplifting or thievery in your place of work. You may equally need to provide more of an essential service or a *moving* product. Whatever the need may be, identify creative ways to create more positive cash flow in your business. With this, you will be able to expand rapidly.

"If you would like to become wealthy, then what you save must earn, and its children must earn, that all may help to give to you the abundance you crave."
- *The Richest Man In Babylon*

III. Business and Financial skills

To succeed in creating multiple streams of income, the last and most important principle I would like to share with you here is the ability to understand numbers. This doesn't mean you need to be a financial or accounting guru to be a successful businessman or woman. In fact, some accounting professionals do a lousy job starting and managing their own businesses.

With understanding the numbers, I mean, your ability to know whether you have made a profit or loss. This is the basic financial skills which many people take for granted.

Your ability to understand a profit and loss statement will help you to read and prepare a *financial report* for your business. To understand *income statement*, you need to be able to differentiate your income from your expenses.

Knowing your assets and liabilities will help you understand a *balance sheet*.

If you improve your knowledge in business and finance, it will help you to better organize your business operations and appreciate the financial dynamics of other businesses in your bid to succeed in creating multiple streams of income from varied business enterprises.

TAKING A JUMP FROM EMPLOYEE TO OWNER

Just as I was about penning down my thoughts under this topic, I chanced on an article by Raya Khashab which outlines in detail all that I needed to say. Raya Khashab Founder of ezClocker, a small business' employee time tracking software, shared his real-life experience of quitting his daytime job and becoming a winner at starting and running a profitable business. Here is what he had to say, "Making the decision to jump from employee to entrepreneur full-time and go "all in" on my own business was one of the hardest and most rewarding experiences of my life.

After working in corporate America for over 15 years, I started my own business, ezClocker. One of the biggest challenges I faced was transitioning from the structured environment of an employee to my new flexible lifestyle as an entrepreneur. The adjustment was hard.

While I always thought I was in control of my time, I often felt like I wasn't actually in control at all. If you're bootstrapping your company like I was, you're likely wearing many hats – for example, you're the one creating the product, talking to customers, and doing the marketing – and it can be overwhelming.

Back then I felt like I was the only one struggling with this career transition, and then I attended a conference that included a fireside chat with broadcast journalist Soledad O'Brien.

She discussed how hectic her schedule had been when she worked for CNN. She would wake up at 4 a.m. every day in order to be at the studio before 6 a.m. Then she wouldn't get home until 5 p.m. or 6 p.m. in the evenings. After spending time with her family and doing chores, she wouldn't get to bed until 11 p.m. or midnight, and then she'd prepare to do it all over again the next day.

Although she admitted that her schedule was crazy back then, it was still a schedule which she followed and didn't have to create herself or even think about.

Today O'Brien has her own media production company, so she gets to make the rules. But she also has the responsibility of setting the priorities for her day and constructing her own schedule. And it turns out that this is sometimes even more challenging and overwhelming than working for a demanding company.

What O'Brien said really hit home for me.

Back in my corporate job, my schedule for most days was already set. Team meetings were scheduled, projects had due dates, and we knew when the busy season was going to come and how long it would last. In addition, I didn't have to worry about marketing campaigns or customer support because we had teams dedicated to that. All I had to do was focus on accomplishing my own tasks.

Eventually, I got better at being my own boss. Here's some advice that helped me transition from employee to entrepreneur:

Take Care of Your Finances

Fear of running out of money and not being able to provide for yourself or your family is one of the biggest reasons people stay at their current job. To conquer this fear, you need to save as much money as you can before making the jump.

But how much is enough? When I was an employee I faced this problem. Do I save enough money for one year? Three years? To help me make a decision I wrote down all of my major monthly expenses – rent, food, cell phone bill, car insurance, health insurance, etc. – and I created a goal to save enough to cover two years' worth of expenses.

Why so much? Because no matter how much you estimate things will cost, you'll inevitably discover that your new company or product takes longer and costs more than you expected.

If you don't have enough savings to cover your expenses for two years, plan to work a few contracting jobs to pay the bills while you reverse roles. Instead of working fulltime and focusing on your startup on the side, work fulltime on your startup and use your nights and weekends for contracting jobs. Taking care of your finances will reduce stress so that you can focus on building your company.

Build Your Support Team

Being an entrepreneur is a lonely journey sometimes, especially if you've worked most of your adult life as an employee. You often don't realize how many other entrepreneurs and friends are employees. It can be hard to relate to.

You'll need to build your support team by surrounding yourself with like-minded people. Join entrepreneur organizations, attend relevant events, and think about utilizing a co-working space. If you don't have an organization for entrepreneurs in your town, consider joining an online group.

In addition to networking with other entrepreneurs, you need mentors for support and advice. When you first start your business, there'll be no shortage of people giving you their words of wisdom – friends, spouses, parents, you name it! Take all that advice with a grain of salt. And when you do choose to listen, be certain it's from a qualified person who has "been there and done that," like a mentor or fellow entrepreneur. Because watching Shark Tank does not make your friend an expert!

Manage Your Time

Time management was one of the most difficult challenges I faced in my transition from employee to entrepreneur. I've found that the following techniques helped me get more control over my time:

Utilize your calendar

Kevin Kruse, the author of 15 Secrets Successful People Know About Time Management, interviewed over 200 ultra-successful people, including 7 billionaires, 13 Olympians, and a host of accomplished entrepreneurs for his book. He says that most successful people don't use a to-do list. Instead, they schedule everything on their calendar. According to Kruse, utilizing your calendar to schedule tasks allows you to free up your mind since you now have a plan for how to address each of your must-do tasks. You can use the calendar to allocate time for things like meetings, writing, exercise, or even time with family and friends.

Build daily routines

Leigh Michaels, the prolific author of more than eight romance novels, once said, "Waiting for inspiration to write is like standing at the airport waiting for a train. Conditions to produce one's craft are rarely ideal, and waiting for everything to be perfect is almost always an exercise in futility." The idea here is that you need to work on your craft every day, even if you don't feel inspired. Build daily routines to help you get organized and reduce stress so that you can achieve this.

After leaving my corporate job, I got into the routine of waking up every day around the same time, even on weekends, so that my body would get accustomed to it.

This allowed me to focus on ezClocker all day without getting tired. I also take breaks throughout the day during which I'll either do a workout or take a walk in the park and listen to a podcast to de-stress and re-energize.

Use Technology

With all the apps and websites on the market today, there's really no excuse not to use them to help you save time and be more productive. Tools like FM help you focus, Workflowy manages your to-do list (if you decide you need one), Sleep Cycle helps you get a better night's sleep, RecurPost helps with Social Media automation, and Asana aids with project management – just to name a few!

Transitioning from employee to entrepreneur is a huge challenge and it can be intimidating, but with the right mindset and a plan, you'll discover strengths and capabilities you never knew you had. As David Viscott said "If you have the courage to begin, you have the courage to succeed." *i*

The grass is always greener on the other side of fear. Taking an entrepreneurial leap of faith is no mean task. The brave often succeeds, leaving behind the masses who are chicken-hearted. Decide to take a jump from employee to business owner today!

UNIT 5

HOW TO START SMALL

Are you below 15 years?

• • • • •

"I made my first investment at age eleven.

I was wasting my life up until then."

Warren Buffet

Childhood is nothing short of living. It is a preparation for adult life. It is life in itself too. We tend to see the period between 1 year and 15 years as a formative stage which needs no critical thinking and decision making on the part of children and teenagers. We, therefore, place little or no responsibility at all on persons within this age bracket.

If you are 15 years or below, you are a perfect individual – you are not a kid. A fifteen-year-old today has already spent 5,473 days, 1,440 minutes and 86,400 seconds of life on earth. If you waste 15 years out of 30 years you have lost 5,473 days, 1,440 minutes and 86,400 seconds of your precious life. If you saved GHC 0.10p (0.048 USD) each day in a penny box (piggy bank) since you were 7 years, you would have saved GHC 292.00 (USD $60.83) by the time you are 15 years old.

The greatest investor of all time Warren Buffet, the third richest man in the world today once said in his advice to young people that, "I made my first investment at age eleven. I was wasting my life up until then."

Are you a teenager or a young adult? Do you feel you have wasted your life?

I want you to chill. Just relax. You have a lot more productive years ahead of you. Time spent can never be recovered. You can only start now to live a great life. There are many successful people in life who wasted their lives until they were 20 years. The truth is that you should be grateful to be enlightened enough to feel the way you feel now.

Today is the right time to put things right. As a child, teenager or young adult, you should think like a winner in life to be one. You do not have to only think like one, you need to act like one.

To be a winner, you must discover for yourself a need or problem in your community and by applying the principles in this book, provide concrete solutions to solve the problems and as well make money for yourself. Business is about solving problems.

In my first book, From Nowhere to Somewhere, you will learn more about yourself, what your true potential is and which area (s) in your life you can make a great impact in, in order to increase your value and be more relevant to society.

I want to share with you a true story of a young man called Farrah Gray who is currently in his thirties. His story has challenged many including myself to demand more from life than just existing or living with no purpose.

THE FARRAH GRAY STORY

Farrah Gray has a net worth of about USD $ 5 million according to research. He is an African American businessman, investor, author and motivational speaker.

He began his entrepreneurial journey at the age of 6 (six). At age six, Farrah Gray was already a 'responsible young adult'. He took responsibility for his own life to make strides towards his future at a very tender age of 6.

Looking at his immediate community, South Side Chicago where he was born and raised by a single mother, young Farrah took to the streets after school to sell painted rocks to his neighbours who used them as door traps.

He also learnt how to make homemade skin lotions which he put out for sale to his community members.

In his book, Reallionare, Nine Steps to Becoming Rich from Inside Out, Farrah Gray recounted that the first money he made was USD $ 9.00 from the sale of his painted rocks. At that time, he saw himself as being USD $999,991 away from being a millionaire.

On his business card at age 9, young Farrah Gray called himself a 21st Century CEO. He went ahead to create a ketchup (tomato ketchup) recipe which he learnt from his grandmother. He sold his ketchup company at the age of 14 years for an amazing USD $ 1.5 million, making him a millionaire.

Success is not only for adults. There are a class of people all over the world like you who are starting small to save, invest and solve problems in their communities to make money and guarantee themselves financial freedom in their immediate future.

Begin today by saving your pennies in a piggy bank. Use all the financial principles in this book which applies to you as well to protect your savings. Soon you can start investing your savings in *solving a problem in your community* (starting a small business) which you could manage while in school.

You need to inform your parents of your intention to be a future millionaire and ask for their prayers and support. Parents should learn to guide their children on this path of entrepreneurship and not discourage them. The best way to learn is by doing. Children need the chance to experiment in the field of entrepreneurship.

All the principles for starting a small business encased in this book are needed for your business success. The best time to have started was 10 years ago. The second best time is now. Begin to be great!

UNIT 6

HOW TO START SMALL

Are you below 30 years?

• • • ••

"Never see yourself as too young to start making important life decisions.

You are actually too ripe not to have started by now."

I.K Adusei

If life were a bone, the period between 20 – 30 years would be the marrow. I believe this is a serious epoch in life and failure to fully utilize all the opportunities that come along with this period will result in dire financial times ahead.

Personally, I founded The ABN Organization at the age of nineteen as a small startup in 2008.

I published my first book, From Nowhere to Somewhere and sold over 1,000 copies at the age of 23.

I bought my first plot of land (80 x 100 plot) at the age of 24. By the age 29 I had purchased over 3.75 acres of land in 3 regions in Ghana, thus Central, Greater Accra and Eastern Region.

I married my beautiful wife who was 24 years at that time at the age 27 years (learn from the central theme of the book/movie *The Great Gatsby* to appreciate the need to marry your life partner early when you find one – not when the time is right).

Larry Page and Sergey Brin of Google, Mark Zuckerberg of Facebook, Steve Jobs of Apple, J.K Rowling of Harry Porter all started to become successful entrepreneurs in their 20's.

One of the people who started their entrepreneurial journey in their twenties is Patrick E. Ngowi.

THE PATRICK NGOWI STORY

Patrick E. Ngowi, is a Tanzanian businessman, public speaker and environmentalist. He is the owner of Helvetic Group which has subsidiaries operating across Africa.

Now 33 years, Patrick received a small loan from his mother worth USD $1,800 to start off Helvetic Solar Contractors Limited, at the age of 22. His company is a pioneer in the supply, installation and maintenance of solar systems throughout the Northern Circuit of Tanzania. His company is the first to provide solar solutions in the Northern Circuit of Tanzania. He started his entrepreneurial endeavour at the age of 15, by selling airtime top-up vouchers in his community. According to Forbes, Helvetic Solar Contractors Limited made USD $3 million in revenue in 2012.

In an interview with Kate Douglas on How We Made It in Africa in 2014, Patrick Ngowi, CEO of Helvetic Group shared his story.

1. What was your first job?

I started doing business while still in school at the tender age of 15 years. I opened my first company before I finished university in China. I have the post as Chairman and CEO of my own company since the age of 22 years. I am now 29 years old.

2. Who has had the biggest impact on your career and why?

My family, especially my mother, has had a huge impact on my career. Being a teacher from rural Tanzania she could only afford to give me US$1,800 as a start-up capital (for Helvetic Group). This was crucial and life-changing. She is now Chairperson of our non-profit foundation, (the Light for Life Foundation).

3. What parts of your job keep you awake at night?

Making my customer happy and satisfied with our service and products. I love making people smile, especially for those that get light for the first time in the rural areas.

4. What are the top reasons why you have been successful in business?

Discipline, trustworthiness, focus, working hard but smart, and most importantly, prayer. The Lord Almighty is my pillar and has brought me so far and the journey still remains long. More prayers needed.

5. What are the best things about your country, Tanzania?

Biodiversity which attracts a growing number of tourists and generates income for the locals.

6. And the worst?

I love my country and the current leadership under President Jakaya Mrisho Kikwete is doing wonders. I applaud him. He is an inspirational leader.

7. Your future career plans?

Helvetic Solar has to scale up operations. With our new strategic approach, keep an eye out for us, not only in Tanzania but in Africa.

8. How do you relax?

I swim, read a lot, run and find time to share with my loved ones.

9. What is your message to Africa's young aspiring business people and entrepreneurs?

Business is a passion. One should find what they love doing, learn as much as they can about it and do business in an open and transparent manner. It is crucial to anticipate vicissitudes, but with passion engrained in their business, one will weather it through.

10. How can Africa realise its full potential?

Africa's potential is in its youth. It remains paramount that investment in youth enterprises, that create more jobs, is done. Local and foreign investors should look closely at youth start-up companies and invest early on. The saying goes, "Those closest to the problems have the best solutions."

My Advice:

Are you under 30?

Never see yourself as too young to start making important life decisions. You are actually too ripe not to have started by now. It is, however, not too late to start afresh and make amends. There are many like you who don't know what you know now.

If you have already started, keep up the good work! Continue being a go-getter. Make yourself and the world proud!

UNIT 7

HOW TO START SMALL

Are you 40 years or below?

● ● ● ● ●

"In business, if you win you win; if you lose, you lose nothing because losing is an essential part of winning!"

I.K Adusei

━━━━━━━━━━━━━━━━━━━━━━━━━

They say *life* begins at forty. Collins dictionary defines life as "the events and experiences that happen to people while they are alive." Judging from this definition, the saying life begins at forty will mean life at forty is no joke. You cannot afford to make mistakes at forty. At forty you should have made all your fatal mistakes in your life else you will have to pay dearly for them.

If you have not learnt all these lessons in this book by forty you should know you are at a critical point in your life right now. At forty, you are at the crossroads of the pit of *hell* and heydays in *heaven*. You will either be driving a four-wheel drive with no knowledge of how expensive fuel costs; be jumping from one *troski* (suburban public transport) to another worried about the cost of transport fares or find yourself somewhere in between.

Life at forty is the defining moment of life. However, if you are below forty there are 5 key lessons you need to know now before you hit forty.

Before you hit forty, you should:

1. Have a plan for your life.

One of the richest men of all time Andrew Carnegie, American Industrialist and Philanthropist, lived a life worthy of emulation. In his recipe for a successful life, he divided life into three.

i. Learn all you can

Life presents you with a lot of lessons most of which we learn unconsciously. According to Andrew Carnegie, there should be a conscious attempt to learn the most you can about what you want to accomplish. You cannot do anything substantial within a field you know nothing about. So use the first trimester of your life to learn as much as you can about what you want to accomplish.

ii. Make all the money you can

Money makes the world go round. If you are young and think money is not important you will soon find out that money is not only important but essential. You need to use your knowledge wisely and time judiciously to solve problems and make money – the most you can.

iii. Give all you can

Andrew Carnegie after amassing the tons of wealth his business acumen brought him, lived the last part of his life giving to charities most especially to the Andrew Carnegie Foundation whose commitment to improving literacy through the setting up of Carnegie Libraries across the world to date long after his demise, is second to none. In Ghana like in many countries across the world, a magnificent portrait of Andrew Carnegie, the American Industrialist, hangs on the wall of Carnegie Reference Library, a department of Balm Library at the University of Ghana, Legon.

If there is anything to learn from the life of Andrew Carnegie who is arguably the wealthiest individual to have ever traversed the surface of the earth, it should be this: *have a plan for your life*, my friend!

2. Know that financial freedom is possible.

Making money is not a bad thing. Building a successful business and solving real-life challenges while putting a smile on the faces of your employees, their families and many others who depend on them is such a refreshing feeling.

Financial stress is what you eliminate from your life if you pursue financial freedom. Never trust the naysayers who belittle your drive to succeed as a start-up entrepreneur. Financial freedom is indeed possible. Never forget that!

3. Know that entrepreneurship is the safest thing that ever happened to humankind – so you should stop playing it safe.

'What if..?' These two words in that order are responsible for the enormity of talents in the graveyard. Many people hold back their possibilities all because of fear of the unknown. Investing in your business idea may not seem safe but the only way to guarantee yourself financial security is if you enjoy business success. The safest way to live your life is to confidently steer your own ship.

Only *doers* will reap the full benefit of this book. You do not learn how to cook by only reading a cookbook. It is apparent that you may fail if you try. After all, in business, if you win you win; if you lose, you lose nothing because losing is an essential part of winning!

4. Know that your bad debt will increase with time.

Debt is not a bad thing, but you should know the difference between good debt and bad debt. *Bad debt* is usually incurred through the procurement of personal loans like student loans, mortgages, auto loans, loans for household appliances etc. With time, the compound interest accruing from such loans will increase significantly. These types of loans should be repaid as soon as possible.

Bad debt can kill you. Bad debt will not make you financially free. It only gets worse with time. Many working class adults have had their lives messed up with the compounding interests on loans procured for personal comfort resulting rather in personal discomfort.

On the other hand, good debt will make you rich. This approach of wealth creation is normally used by sophisticated investors. If you prudently use bank loans to invest in properties that generate more positive cash flow to pay off such loans, you will be using good debt to create assets which will make you filthy rich.

Knowing the difference between good debt and bad debt is required in your quest to win big in business and in life.

5. Know that you are in control of your destiny.

One day or day one?

The greatest lie ever told by people especially many below the ages of forty and fifty is that one day the goddess of good fortune will cross their path and suddenly everything they touch will turn into gold.

Many people believe in this lie. They, therefore, continue to hold back, expectant of the day the goddess of good fortune will finally cross their path.

The greatest truth is that you are in control of your destiny. You can wait for one day to be successful or take today as day one, to become a man or woman of value.

When you get to understand that your destiny is the result of your own choices, you will witness the amazing power of personal growth; you will know that the key to success lies in utilizing your God-given potential to the fullest. Take charge of your own future. The best time is NOW!

UNIT 8

HOW TO START SMALL

Are you 40 years or above?

• • • • •

"Life begins at forty!"

Unknown

_____

$\mathcal{T}$he statement life begins at forty falls short of being literal. It is a very profound statement which carries a myriad of life offers. At forty there are many people on their third or second gear of success and triumph in business and in life. There are others who are facing mid-life crises. The reality of life, the burden and the pressures thereof begin at forty. If you are above forty, you know what I'm talking about.

Nonetheless, according to a survey conducted in the US and presented by the Kauffman Foundation, the percentage of entrepreneurs between the ages of 45 to 54 increased from 25.2 per cent in 2003 to 30 per cent in 2013.[ii]

This shows that many people over forty are having a field day in running their own businesses. Starting small and succeeding in style is after all not the preserve of the youth and young adults below forty.

The conditions leading to starting a business and succeeding in style differ greatly when one crosses the forty line. There is, therefore, the need to take cognisance of those particular conditions which support the growth of businesses by entrepreneurs over forty years.

I have had an encounter with many people of varied age ranges, life experiences and lessons. I have learnt over the years that the statement life begins at forty is the truest life warning or advice ever given. However, there are many advantages for people over forty who venture in business.

ADVANTAGES OF STARTING A BUSINESS AFTER FORTY

If you are above forty you may have witnessed a lot of real-life challenges which include false start and failure in most aspects of your life. It is a normal occurrence. This real-life experience will be needed in the area of entrepreneurship after forty.

Here are the advantages of starting a business after forty.

1. Caution

In real estate, there is an old aged Latin saying which reads, *caveat emptor* which is translated in English to mean *buyers beware*! At forty it is believed that you have put an end to what we call youthful exuberance which results in haste and lack of attention to detail in business and in life. A forty to sixty-year-old who wants to venture into business would mostly have the benefit of hindsight in all the enterprises he or she may invest his money or time in.

Combined with financial literacy and prudent business practices, caution can help a middle-aged entrepreneur to navigate smoothly through the entrepreneurial waters. Caution used here refers to carefulness, restraints, thoughtfulness and attentiveness.

2. Focus

By virtue of youthfulness and thought of having more productive lives ahead, most people below forty waste their time moving from one quickie business to another. The desire to get quick results forces the youth and some young adults to abandon projects which would have ended up generating more profit in a short or medium term. An utter lack of focus in business is symptomatic of most business failures among youth businesses.

At forty, there is no time for trial and error. Middle-aged adults, therefore, are more careful in choosing businesses that guarantee a steady profit to keep them going. Focusing on such businesses and patiently scaling it up can result in financial success.

3. Resources

It is easier for middle-aged adults to have access to financial resources than someone at age 25. It is assumed that between 30 to 45 years one may have had the opportunity to work and save some cash. It is equally possible for these people to have access to bank loans and other assets like lands, houses and other properties which they may have acquired or inherited from their family relations.

These resources when carefully utilized can help make money available to start a business, acquire an existing business or invest in one as a partner. This situation predisposes middle-aged adults to a better chance of starting their own businesses.

4. Family

The family is the bedrock of society. The success or failure of business always takes its root from the home. Middle-aged or retired married couples who commit their time and resources to venture into a viable business will have a greater chance of business success. It takes two to tango. When there is enough mutual understanding, commitment and focus among married couple especially over forty, the family can be a haven for business success.

5. Network

Your network is your net worth is an old aged cliché which has never dropped its value. The size of one's network can be as priceless as a chest of gold. This may include contacts made at work, conferences, seminars, churches, trips, family relations and acquaintances etc. Age comes with a repertoire of such priceless contacts. Conscious use of your network can save you a lot of money which you would have otherwise spent out of your pocket.

UNIT 9

HOW TO START SMALL

The Business Mindset Theory

● ● ● ● ●

"Whether you think you can or you can't, either way,
you are right."

Henry Ford

*B*usiness is for though minds. The business terrain is always a challenge. Money doesn't grow on trees as they say, yet you can make your business a tree which sprouts out money every day.

The word business was first used in the 18th century. It originated from the old English word *bisignis* which means anxiety. It was initially used to connote the *state of being busy*, thus *busyness*. *Bisignis* is associated with words like *care, anxiety, occupation, diligence* etc.

With this vivid etymology of the word business, no one can succeed in business with the mindset of it being a less serious activity. Business is a serious undertaking.

WORKING HARD VRS WORKING SMART

Hard work pays!

When you sample the views of 100 business leaders in this world, 100% of them will advise aspiring entrepreneurs to prepare themselves for hard work.

However, this advice doesn't hold true when you ask these same men about the main ingredient for business success.

Bill Gates, the second richest man in the world as I write today, once said, "I choose a lazy person to do a hard job. Because a lazy person will find an easy way to do it."

In essence, building a successful business requires the ability to find an easy way to solve big world challenges.

Arguably, laziness brought about the invention of machines and equipment. For years strongmen (strong labourers) were needed to dig a deep foundation for a high rise building. Till now, this is still the case in most parts of Africa and other emerging economies.

On the other hand, smart entrepreneurs including Bill Gates continue to think of smart and easy ways to solve world problems.

Today, there are many earth-moving machines, tools and heavy equipment which can dig deep foundations and put up high rise buildings in few days as opposed to the many harrowing days of building such structures using manpower.

Working hard has its place. It connotes tenacity of purpose, resilience and focus. This notwithstanding, successful entrepreneurs succeed by accomplishing a hard task in an easier, faster and more efficient way. Smart work always beats hard work when hard work is not smartly done.

THE MANET GROUP STORY

"Dr. Mrs. Theresa Oppong – Berko is the President of Manet Group, the second largest real estate developer in Ghana and the diversified office/residential and hotel accommodation provider. Over the years, her company has played an active role in the real estate industry.

Immediately after earning a Bachelor of Arts degree in Political Science and Sociology from the University of Ghana, Legon in 1985, she went into her first business venture – fishing and failed, leaving her with debt equivalent to USD$ 2.5 million at the age of 25. Feeling unlettered in business, she went back to Legon, acquired a Masters' Degree in Business Administration (where she was declared Best Marketing Student in 1990) and then began pursuing her real dream of constructing buildings.

The company has built over 1,200 residential units, a three-star hotel resort, and other civil engineering facilities such as urban roads, motor carriages, bypasses, just to mention a few. Dr. Theresa Oppong – Berko brings a refreshing whiff of fresh air to this, usually colourless, notoriously male-dominated industry.

In 1998, she established Manet Hotels Limited, which acquired a beach resort at Ada, just outside of Accra and developed it into a three-star, 48 room hotel with an amazing array of recreational and leisure activities on offer including Acqua sport and marlin fishing. It is now fittingly known as Manet Paradise.

She is blazing an entrepreneurial trail in Ghana's real estate industry that is proving hard, near impossible for her private sector counterparts to follow.

Today, she sits astride the huge Manet Group, which comprises Manet Housing, a real estate development firm, Manet Construction, a civil engineering company; and Manet Towers. MANET Properties was presented with the overall property award for 2012 dubbed 'Property Walk of Fame" at the 5th Ghana Property Awards." - *Careers Ghana*

Business is a mindset. Once you have the tenacity of purpose and willingness to go the extra mile to succeed, nothing can stop you from achieving success in your business venture. Losing in business is an essential part of winning! If you win you win if you lose, you learn.

Always remember, successful entrepreneurs, succeed by accomplishing a hard task in an easier, faster and more efficient way. *Smart work always beats hard work when hard work is not smartly done*!

UNIT 10

HOW TO START SMALL

Are you ready to succeed?

• • • • •

"Some people dream of success, while other people get up every morning and make it happen."

Wayne Huizenga

Starting a business is one of the few most refreshing feelings life will ever bring to you. It is an honourable duty to bring to life that which never were.

It is a beautiful piece of art which you create using resources from your imagination, intuition and knowledge - summed up as your creativity.

A perfect acronym for *im*agination, *in*tuition and *k*nowledge is *I'm INK*.

As an entrepreneur, you are the ink of your craft. The products or services you provide are the writings, scribbles or sketches from your ink.

Imagination, whisked together with intuition and knowledge uncovers the depth of your creativity – also referred as *I'm INK* in the form of an acronym. All the businesses you find today were brewed in the pots of someone or a group of people's creativity.

So you need to know that the people at the top did not fall there. They took time to develop their imagination, intuition and knowledge.

Among these three compositions of your creativity, two of them are free and made available to humans at birth. These are imagination and intuition. Knowledge, on the other hand, is acquired consciously. According to psychologists, human beings are born tabula rasa (with blank memory). The extent of human altitude is therefore in direct correlation with one's cognitive or physical aptitude.

Say this to yourself: As an entrepreneur or a small business owner, I'M INK! The scribbles, scrawls or writings I make (ie. the products and services I provide) are a direct reflection of the depth of my imagination, intuition and knowledge.

IMAGINATION IS KEY

Imagination is the playground of the mind. Children are not afraid to use their imagination. It is a part of your life which gives you free access to limitless possibilities. Few people use their imagination in today's world. The youth of today and young adults alike do little altogether to deplete their imagination reserves. Adults are preoccupied with daily challenges and increasing exigencies of life. They, therefore, fail to sit back and plan their lives adequately using the power of their imagination.

Whenever you stop to take a look at the things around you including the malls, skyscrapers, latest technology, cars, bullet trains, etc., you need to ask yourself what you have used your imagination to create. This may sound too sharp and straight forward but this book is here to do nothing less than that. This book is to help you know how much value you have and to guide you on the path to starting small and winning big in business and in life.

So now, ask yourself this question again, what have you created with your imagination?

INTUITION IS KING

Other words synonymous to intuition are awareness, sensitivity, clairvoyance, insight, gut, instinct, the sixth sense, etc.

The sixth sense is a very important contributory factor to the success of any major decision making. Wikipedia defines intuition *as the ability to acquire knowledge without proof, evidence, or conscious reasoning or without understanding how the knowledge was acquired.* Intuition comes from the Latin verb *intueri* translated as "consider" or from the late Middle English word *intuit*, "to contemplate". Intuition has also been described as the ability to understand something instinctively, without the need for conscious reasoning.

An entrepreneur in describing how he uses his intuition in his business did recount, *"I rely on my gut instincts all the time in my work with clients. Part of my job is to bring order and structure to the thoughts and behaviours of others. To do that, I channel my tendencies as an empathic and highly sensitive person. I also tap into my*

intuition, which helps me get to the source of what's troubling someone - even if they can't find the words themselves."

Intuition usually involves trusting the collection of past *subconscious* experiences. It is therefore believed that those exposed to more experiences in a particular field will have a lot of repertoire of intuition to draw from. However, intuition exists in the subconscious memory and cannot be acquired through a conscious learning process.

Intuition is needed a lot, especially in making critical business decisions. Whatever your intuition will be in a particular situation, it will be proven right or wrong in the quality of decisions you make.

KNOWLEDGE IS A CAUSE

In my first book **From Nowhere to Somewhere: How A Solid Vision Can Change Your Whole Life** which is selling fast on amazon.com, I shared some strong views on knowledge as I have come to know it to be:

"Knowledge is a cause, any other thing is the effect. There is nothing created by man without knowledge. It is, therefore, revealing that man cannot identify what exactly he can do with his life without being exposed to the knowledge of things. Knowledge makes up a man, and lack of it is man's greatest limitation.

The dynamics of various societies reflects greatly the kind of knowledge and exposure its members have had overtime. Societies more exposed to technology, science and exploration evidently churn out inventors, space explorers, astronauts, cars and aeroplane manufacturers, name them. Members of these societies arguably are not asked to act the way they do but rather, their thoughts and actions are informed by what their societies expose them to.

Alternatively, societies with the predominance of entrenched and unamenable culture, tradition, mysticism and superstition bring forth members who are less motivated to progress due to their conservative nature and their lack of interest to pursue knowledge."

Knowledge is the real currency of the world. A day without adding more knowledge to your knowledge bank will mean an eventual loss of opportunity tomorrow. The knowledge acquired today, for instance, has the potential to increase the money in your bank account tomorrow.

To start small and become successful you need to know your stuff. You need to have in-depth knowledge of your chosen business venture. Your ability to be current about the daily happenings in the financial system you operate in, as well as that of your immediate business climate will help in your decision making which will reflect in the overall performance of your business.

In the area of knowledge, your worth today is indicative of how much of it you possess in all areas of your life.

Your understating or knowledge of money, for instance, is reflective of the size of your bank account or your asset portfolio.

Reading this book to this point means that you are predisposed to the quest for more knowledge. Success and riches await you. Keep pursuing knowledge! The room for improvement is never full.

At the utmost, learn to take action!

AT ALL COST AVOID THE RAT RACE

Image Credit/EntrepreneurMindset

UNIT 11

HOW TO START SMALL

Why Start Small?

• • • • •

"As an entrepreneur, your business can only get BIG if
you have enough patience to start small."

I.K Adusei

I learnt from Robert Kiyosaki, my mentor from afar, in
his book Rich Dad Poor Dad that, his best friend's
father who was his *rich dad* taught him to go to school,
get good grades and find a good company to buy. As a
business enthusiast, you also have the options to start

small, grow organically to the point you can take your business public – thus to be publicly listed on your country's stock exchange or other countries' stock exchange.

To be able to buy a good company and keep it successful or profitable, your first task will be to know how to start a business from scratch and make it attractive to potential investors and financiers.

I usually ask this question on the many platforms I get to speak on the subject of How to Start Small, "What would you do with USD $ 10 million if your grandfather bequeathed you such an inheritance?"

The answer has never been that which relate to spending all the money (USD$ 10 million in total) on my audiences business ideas or their current businesses. I always find on their expenditure list, unrelated matters including, travel, clothing, family needs, leisure, food, mansions, luxury cars etc. even when I drop the figure from USD$ 10 million to USD$ 100,000.

This reveals the fact that many people will waste money on frivolous expenditure whenever they are given monies outside what they can actually work with in their business ventures.

By inference, small businesses do not need, USD$ 100,000 if they cannot fully or effectively use USD$ 1,000 when given one.

It will be expedient to start with GHC 500 or GHC 1,000 to grow and expand using prudent business practices and financial know-how than to borrow GHC 20,000 to start a business which you have no experience in handling as far as running your business is concerned.

FASTEST WAY TO SUCCEED IN BUSINESS IS TO START SMALL

Ironically, the fastest way to succeed in business is to start small.

Aeroplanes, rockets and spaceships are more agile than any other machine ever made to traverse the surface of the earth. However, none of these sky-moving machines ever achieves full cruise altitude the moment the engine is turned on.

According to research, a standard aeroplane will first have to move sturdily along the runway to line up with the flight path before it speeds a bit faster on the runway to gain momentum to be able to finally begin a head-on flight into the sky.

Even after covering a long distance on the ground before taking off, research shows that a standard jet-aircraft, for example, an A340 or 777 will take about 20 minutes (1,200 seconds) to climb to cruise altitude, at an average ground speed of 200 knots.

Hence, the aircraft will cover about 70 miles in 20 minutes, two times slower (on the ground) than the distance it would have covered in the sky if the same jet-aircraft had attained its cruise altitude.

Aeroplanes fly unhurriedly on the ground over long distances just to gain momentum to be able to fly at cruise altitude. Similarly, businesses can learn a lot from the process of flying an aircraft.

As an entrepreneur, your business can only get BIG if you have enough patience to start small.

THE COCA-COLA STORY

"In 1886, Coca-Cola was invented by a Pharmacist named John Pemberton, otherwise known as "Doc". He fought in the Civil War, and at the end of the war, he decided he wanted to invent something that would bring him commercial success.

Usually, everything he made failed in pharmacies. He invented many drugs, but none of them ever made any money. So after a move to Atlanta, Pemberton decided to try his hand in the beverage market.

In his time, the soda fountain was rising in popularity as a social gathering spot. Temperance was keeping patrons out of bars so making a soda – fountain drink (soft drink) just made sense.

And this was when Coca-Cola was born. However, Pemberton had no idea how to advertise. This is where Frank Robinson came in. He registered Coca-Cola's formula with the patent office and he designed the logo. He also wrote the slogan, "The Pause That Refreshes."

Coke did not do so well in its first year. And to make matters worse, Doc Pemberton died in August in 1888, meaning he would never see the commercial success he had been seeking.

After Pemberton's death, a man named Asa Griggs Candler rescued the business. In 1891 he became the sole owner of Coca-Cola. It was when Candler took over that one of the most innovative marketing techniques was invented. He hired travelling salesmen to pass out coupons for a free Coke. His goal was for people to try the drink, like it, and buy it later on. In addition to the coupons, Candler also decided to spread the word of Coca-Cola by plastering logos on calendars, posters, notebooks and bookmarks to reach customers on a large stage. It was one step in making Coca-Cola a national brand, rather than just a regional brand." [iii]

It will surprise you to know that from its inception on May 8, 1886, Coca-Cola only sold 25 *gallons* of syrup in its first year.

Fast forward to the year 2000, Coca-Cola became the top-ranked soft drink in the United States. 2006 saw Coca-Cola and Coca-Cola Enterprises being ranked No.1 and No. 2 on Fortunes 500 list of best beverage and best beverage company respectively.

Today, the Coca-Cola brand is worth over USD $ 79 billion ranking 3rd as the world's largest food company according to the recent 2017 Forbes Global 2000 rankings.

With resilience and tenacity of purpose, your small business today will tomorrow climb high to attain world rankings.

---

iii http://iml.jou.ufl.edu/projects/spring08/Cantwell/invention.html

UNIT 12

HOW TO START SMALL

Checklist For Starting A Business &

Succeeding In Style

#1: IDEA

Ideas rule the world.

– Napoleon Bonaparte

You cannot start anything of value without an idea. As we move about each day, our minds are encumbered with thousands of ideas.

Businesses are built out of a simple idea. This idea could be generated from various sources. The key here is that any *good idea* is worth writing down. I have come to learn that, good ideas are usually stubborn and will disappear shortly after their visit when they are not written down.

Keeping a diary, notebook or notepad close to you wherever you may be is a very smart way to keep track of your ideas. Your breakthrough business idea may simply be a pen and notepad away. You can as well make good use of your smartphones. There are notebook or notepad apps you can download to keep track of your ideas as and when they come. You only have to make sure your phone has efficient battery life. In the past, I had instances where my phone went off when I had a good idea to jot down.

Ideas, however, become relevant only when they are used or applied. There is no use piling up business ideas in your diary only to find out years later that someone has a similar idea and is implementing it in your area.

You never know when you will be encountered with a good idea but here are five ways to generate great ideas.

5 WAYS TO GENERATE GREAT IDEAS

1. Be Observant:

Whenever you have the opportunity to travel or to visit a new place, be an active observer not a passive one. Be open and observe the changes and novelty around you. People who grow up in developing countries are mostly discouraged from openly observing new things.

There are instances when children are made to shy away from glancing through the windows of cars to look at buildings, new places, beautiful artefacts or even passer-by celebrities while in public transport with their parents. This is seen as an uncouth behaviour by some parents. By their standards, staring at things like that in the open constitute a *philistine* behaviour. This behaviour of parents inadvertently has resulted in most people's inability to appreciate the art of observation. Even as adults, they travel to new places without taking notice of any new development around them. They behave like everything is normal and yet they know little or next to nothing about anything.

According to Albert Einstein, *you can live your life as though nothing is a miracle or as if everything is a miracle.* You cannot have a light bulb idea with your eyes closed. Light bulb (great) ideas are all around us. Those who are observant and appreciative of nature and change are those who are able to see and take advantage of them. One of those very observant few is Mark Zuckerberg, Founder of Facebook.

The Facebook Idea

As a fresher (freshman) at Harvard, Mark Zuckerberg realised that the only way to get more information about his colleagues online was to go through the school's website. The Harvard website at the time had a catalogue of students with their photos and some scanty information about them. The students' details provided were limited to halls of residence. Detailed students' profiles were not *accessible* online. So Mark decided to better the students' profiles online. So he created facebook.com which was launched in 2004.

Zuckerberg today continue to rake in billions from a simple observation. Facebook today according to Bloomberg is worth over USD $ 400 billion.

A simple observation can make you a billionaire too. What are you observing?

2. Read More

Being current is the currency of today. The more information you are exposed to, the broader your view of the world and things around you. You can travel to the four corners of the world in the pages of the books you read.

There are many stories of people having light bulb moments while flipping through the pages of books they chanced on.

The more you expose yourself to knowledge and experience, new ideas in your area of interest will keep popping up.

You can only start small in a specific business venture if you can bear the pain of reading many pages of books related to such a business.

3. Socialize

I have met a lot of people who bless their stars for having met me. Most of them claim that their lives have had a massive turn around after having an encounter with me. I can say the same with my encounter with other people in my life.

Moving out of your comfort zone can present you with the business idea you have always been waiting for. Sometimes what is on the other side of the road is worth seeing. The party next door, the old student association meeting, the outdooring event, the sod cutting event, the book launch, the keep fit event, etc. are all worth attending. When you socialize, you meet new people, you develop a new perspective of things, and you get exposed to new ideas and new ways of doing things. Staying in your little corner can only take you so far. Who knows, you may encounter your million dollar business idea if you make the effort to socialize more.

4. Go for a Walk

As a small business owner or an aspiring entrepreneur, you need to know what is going on in your immediate vicinity. By going for a walk you can make use of all the above-mentioned ways of generating ideas. You can observe, socialize, take note and be able to read more about new developments in your neighbourhood.

The more conversant you are of your vicinity, the better ideas you can generate to make your business stand out.

To start small and smart, going for a walk or jogging around your neighbourhood is a smart way to generate new ideas to lead your business on the path to success.

5. Meditate

Some ideas are buried deep down in your subconscious memory. They are treasures kept for your use. Most people do not take time off their daily busy schedules to have quiet times or meditate.

You need a break to have communion with yourself. You need to evaluate yourself and know your key strength and weaknesses. This period of meditation or introspection can afford you the opportunity to develop new ideas, aspire for new challenges, stop bad and harmful habits and put you on a new path for progress in all aspects of your life.

BUSINESS IDEA TRACKER

At this point of your encounter with this book, have you come across any business idea (s)?

Put them down! An idea well written down has its value priced in *gold*. An idea not written down is a potential USD $1 million loss.

NO.	DATE/ TIME	BUSINESS IDEA	DESCRIPTION
Eg.	20/04/18 13:36 pm	Build a social network	I want to create a social network to link students and teachers all over the world.
1.			
2.			
3.			
4.			
5.			

6.			
7.			
8.			
9.			
10.			
11.			
12.			
13.			
14.			
15.			
16.			
17.			
18.			
19.			
20.			

#2: BRAINSTORM

*Any man who reads too much and **uses his own brain too little** falls into lazy habits of thinking.*

– Albert Einstein

The Business Dictionary defines brainstorming as *a process of generating creative ideas and solutions through intensive and freewheeling group discussion.* Here every participant is encouraged to think aloud and suggest as many ideas as possible, no matter how outlandish or weird those ideas may be.

To start small and grow big, you need to start right. Most budding entrepreneurs require inputs from individuals and people who are having relevant skills and competencies in key areas of their business. In such cases, you need to find a way to invite the inputs of such persons without compromising the safety of your business idea.

I have had people call me on various occasions to pick my brain on a wide range of business issues mostly to flesh out their own business ideas. I actually do not have a problem contributing to someone else's business success whenever my inputs are needed. At some point, however, people will have to pay for such services.

Successful use of this brainstorming technique can help you get ahead and excel quicker than wasting precious time on a business you know little about. Shrewd entrepreneurs are able to create a mastermind brainstorming group without the members knowing exactly which businesses they want to start. They seek for relevant inputs among key sector players in an indirect and subtle manner to avoid the feeling of exploitation on the part of technical brains.

On the other hand, certain types of businesses require active players who you have to bring on board as team players. Such businesses like tech businesses including, fintech, blockchain technology etc require a close business partner with whom you can brainstorm on a daily basis to be able to get your business up and running. In the tech space, for instance, Larry Page of Google needed Sergey Brin, Steve Jobs of Apple needed Steve Wozniak,

Bill Gates of Microsoft needed Paul Allen, and the list goes on. You may need a strategic business partner who will complement your skill or ability to develop and successfully execute your idea.

Today, Jack Ma, Founder of Alibaba, the second largest online selling (e-commerce) platform that had revenue of more than USD$ 8 billion for the third quarter of 2018 alone, may be the king of brainstorming technique. His company Alibaba was foundered in 1999 together with 18 founders. As a school teacher who did not have enough technical knowledge in computer software or programming, Ma was able to surround himself with a tech-savvy brainstorming and mastermind group to set up what has become the biggest e-commerce company second only to Amazon – the US-based e-commerce colossus. In some of his brainstorming sessions, Jack Ma would ask his team to *stand upside down* to keep their brains refreshed and their bodies energized. Brainstorming has proven itself to be a powerful tool for organizing one's business idea for a more efficacious output.

3 KEYS TO SUCCESSFUL BRAINSTORMING

> *"You can design and create, and build the most wonderful place in the world.*
>
> *But it takes people to make the dream a reality."*
>
> – Walt Disney

1. Quantity Over Quality

In brainstorming over a subject – in this case, your business idea, the focus should not be on the quality of the thought, feelings and opinions of your participants. Participants here are a team of experts or colleagues with relevant skills for the session. In any case, the moderator (the person calling for the brainstorming session or any other person he/she may appoint) is equally a participant in the brainstorming session.

A brainstorming session is done by asking for the opinions of participants on the main subject presented for brainstorming.

In moderating a successful brainstorming session, the focus should be on creating a pool of plans, options, ideas, approaches or activities out of which the desired outcome may pop up. The more inputs made by participants, the better and richer the output needed. Quality of thoughts should make way for quantity of thought. This will provide access to the most valuable inputs which may be a second or third guess of your participants.

2. Types of Approaches

There are two main types of brainstorming techniques available for entrepreneurs who want to start small.

These are overt (direct) approach and covert (indirect) approach.

In Overt/Direct Brainstorming sessions, participants are made aware of their participation in the session in order to achieve the desired objective. Participants here are usually partners or stakeholders in the business venture. This requires participants to be physically present at the venue designated for the brainstorming. It could be in an office, home or an outdoor venue.

In Covert/Indirect Brainstorming sessions, the participants are not made aware of the original motive behind the topic for brainstorming. The moderator usually has a one-on-one encounter with his or her participants and ask pertinent questions demanding their respective inputs. This line of brainstorming could be done over time, engaging a cross-section of participants until the desired information is retrieved or realized for onward decision making.

3. How to Execute

The moderator of a brainstorming session should adopt a laissez-*faire* attitude in moderating the session. If you are the one calling for a brainstorming session over a particular business idea or strategy, it will be advisable to allow the participants to freely communicate their opinions and thoughts. It will be counter-productive to be interjecting and providing counter-arguments to defend a certain position against another.

#3. FIND A PURPOSE OR CAUSE

Without purpose, you achieve nothing.

– I.K Adusei

I hold the aforementioned opinion strongly. Truly, without purpose, we achieve nothing. You cannot start a business without having a purpose for undertaking that business. You cannot just follow the entrepreneurship bandwagon and go ahead and set up any business.

Your motive for setting up a business should be made clear from the start. We set up businesses to achieve a desired aim or fulfil a specific need.

Nokia phones were designed and manufactured to *connect people*. Aliko Dangote set up the Dangote Group to help Nigeria and Africa to *substitute imports with quality Nigerian products*. Oprah Winfrey set up the Oprah Winfrey Network to give *voice to the voiceless*. Robert Kiyosaki's Rich Dad Company is set up to provide *financial literacy to the masses*. This book, How to Start Small is to *help readers start small and win big in business and in life*. The ABN Organization is set up to *build globally competitive businesses in Africa*.

You need to find a purpose which inspires your business pursuit. Running a business can be very overwhelming and frustrating since real success doesn't come overnight.

Every solid business purpose is firmly rooted in an individual's life purpose. For example, I never dream of being a professional sumo wrestler. My business purpose will definitely have little or nothing to do with sumo wrestling as far as I know.

Your life purpose always finds a way to fit into your business purpose. For you to succeed in business and in life, you cannot be tied to a business which you are not fond of. You can only go so far with a business which you do not have an interest in, you do not love or simply do not find yourself engaging in, in the future. If you find yourself in any of such businesses, you are bound to fail.

Steve Jobs is the Founder of Apple. As I write Apple's stock has grown so much, making Apple the first USD $ 1 trillion company in the world.

Which lesson can we learn from Steve Jobs (1955-2011)? This is what he had to say about finding your life and business purpose.

In a speech delivered at Stanford University, Steve Jobs opined, *"You have to find what you love. And that is as true for your work as it is for your lovers. Your work is going to fill a large part of your life, and the only way to be truly satisfied is to do what you believe is great work.*

And the only way to do great work is to love what you do. If you haven't found it yet keep looking. Don't settle. As all matters of the heart, you'll know when you find it. And, like any relationship, it just gets better as the years roll on. So keep looking until you find it. Don't settle!

Your time is limited, so don't waste it living someone else's life. Don't be trapped by dogma – which is living with the results of other people's thinking. Don't let the noise of others' opinions drown out your own inner voice. And most importantly, have the courage to follow your heart and intuition. They somehow already know what you truly want to become. Everything else is secondary."

As Steve asserted in his speech, finding a purpose for life or a particular business doesn't usually present itself as an easy task.

Nonetheless, engaging your thoughts in answering the following questions can help you establish your purpose for life and by extension a purpose for your business.

1. What do you love doing?

You can establish a business and be more successful if you know what you love doing. Business, as we have learnt earlier on, is from the old English word *bisignis* which means anxiety. It was similarly used in the 18th century to refer to *busyness* – thus being busy. I do not want to recommend a business which will make you so anxious and busy that, you would die off quickly when you hit

your first million. So find what you love doing most, and find a way to make money from it. It is as simple as that.

2. What kind of people do you love to be around?

I have come across a lot of people who have on repeat this chorus in their homes, churches, cars and even funeral grounds, "I hate my job." The kind of people you find around you, wherever you are, may either uplift your spirit or lower it into the blazing pit of hell. If you love to be around footballers, craft a business around football and get to work. You will be more successful and more importantly have a long happy life.

3. If time, money, energy and talent were unlimited, what would you do with your life?

This may be a very tricky question. But grab yourself a cool drink of your choice and make sure you are in your favourite restaurant with a cosy environment and cool background music. Try to answer this question in that mood and you are sure to have an accurate answer. Once you get an answer, your work will be to structure a business around that. Trust me you will be successful! It works.

4. Who are the people you greatly admire?

The people you admire, admire you too. The business you are looking for is looking for you. Stop dreaming and get to work. Be yourself!

5. What is the common thread that runs through your answers?

In answering these questions you may have picked up a common thread which runs through the answers you gave. If you have answered all these questions, by now you should know what your business purpose is.

Complete this:

My life purpose is…………………………..……………..…

My greatest skill in business is …..…………………………

The business I run (or want to run is) …………………….

The purpose of this business is…………………………..…

The vision I have for this business is ……………….....…

#4. BUSINESS PLAN

Investopedia defines a business plan in its simplest form as *a written down document that describes in detail how a new business is going to achieve its goals*. A business plan may also include background information about the organization or team attempting to achieve those goals.

You do not need a written business plan to start your business. However, it is a basic requirement for you to properly organize your business and particularly open up your business for potential financiers and partners.

Irrespective of how long your business has been in operation you need to have a business plan. A well-drafted business plan can help you secure funding for your start-up business or expand your business operation.

Why get a business plan?

Any business looking to raise a loan, approach an investor or decide to source funds from venture capitalists, needs to have a business plan.

A loan officer, for instance, is mostly interested in your business' ability to repay the loan on time. A well-documented business plan which details healthy financial projections and having a solid strategy to achieve sales goals will help you access the bank loan your business requires.

Investors and venture capitalists, on the other hand, are typically interested in Return on Investment (ROI). Your business plan should, therefore, be able to demonstrate your business' ability to guarantee them a return on their investment and the ability to generate steady positive cash flow for your business.

A detailed *good corporate management system* along with a well-demonstrated potential for scaling up your business will be a massive win for you if you approach investors.

Beyond searching for funds for your business, a good business plan will help you organize your business in the area of sales, access to market, provide a solid business direction and also help segment your operations.

A few years ago I read about a survey by a software company in the United States on the relevance of a business plan to your business. The company surveyed its users to discover how relevant a business plan is to their business success. The findings were presented to the University of Oregon for validation. The outcome of the survey seemed to suggest the affirmative. Business plans contributed significantly to the success of those who had one.

Of those who created business plans, 64% had business growth. Of those without a finished business plan, only 43% had business growth.

Those who had written business plans were more likely to secure loans to grow their businesses than those without one.

COMPONENTS OF A BUSINESS PLAN

The main components of a business plan include:

1. Executive Summary

An executive summary as its name suggests summarises the key elements of your business plan in a short space. Your business summary should be like a 'mini skirt'. It should be short and relevant but long enough to cover the valuable assets. Any attempt to overemphasize the key elements of your business plan in your executive summary will throw your pitch out of gear, making your business plan unattractive.

So please note that your executive summary should distil all the important information in a reasonably short space.

2. Business Description

Business description offers you an avenue to market your story. Here you generally talk about how your business started, the year you started, the problem you intend to solve, how you intend to solve it, your business model, business location and your projected growth.

You can start with a short catchy story of the needs assessment, thus the need you see in your community, country or the world at large, how you feel about it and how you intend turning it around to make a profit (in case it is a profit motive business) or to benefit your target group (if it is a non-profit or charity).

You proceed to state your business model or approach to solving the problem at hand, then the legal structure or framework within which you operate. It is also prudent to attach your business location and your competitive advantage or edge you have over your competitors.

You need to note the key points enumerated above and know that your business description presents to your potential lenders, partners or investors your own view of your business.

3. Market Analysis

A savvy businessman/woman knows his/her market. An effective analysis of your market hones your understanding of the market you operate in. Market analysis is an exercise in seeing where you fit in the market and where you stand among your competitors.

4. Management Team

The organization management section of your business plan affords you the opportunity to talk about your team superstars. People in business know that the quality of your team has a telling effect on the efficiency of your product and service delivery.

So use this opportunity to project the skills, qualification, experience and uniqueness of your team. Your ability to do this well will lift the image of your company and the value of your brand to potential stakeholders.

5. Sales Strategies

How do you intend making money with your business? How do you stay profitable? Your sales strategy should outline your unique approach to turning doubters into believers of your brand or business.

A well-composed sales strategy should explain your pricing strategy – and how that can drive sales up to the roof. It should include your promotional strategies – both current and future, which you deem fit to execute in order to win and keep your customers.

It should also have your online sales approach. The use of search engine optimization, effective use of social media and your implementation strategies are key.

6. Budgeting

To attract potential investors, lenders and venture capitalist, your business operations and projections should have a cost element to it.

You should clearly outline the cost of every item, system or strategy you are going to use to achieve your objectives. Having an annual or five-year budgeting plan broken down into yearly requirements will make potential stakeholders appreciate the extent of risk they are taking vis-à-vis the financial rewards they are entitled to.

7. Financial Projections

You start your financial projections with the successes you have chalked financially till this point. If you have any previous financial success in your business, you will have great potential for financial injections from investors and lenders for the growth and expansion of your business.

Nonetheless, you should have a robust forecast of the returns envisaged for the future based on your sales strategies and a careful analysis of your market trend. For more accurate financial projections, there should also be a true assessment of your business position. It should be noted that the key to the financial success of your establishment lies in your strategic investments in staff, equipment and service delivery.

#5: NO BUSINESS PLAN

Whoever told you that you cannot succeed in business without a written business plan is a lair. Actually, do you really need a written business plan to start a business? The question can be asked a million times and the answer will always be NO!

You do not need to have a business plan to succeed in business. There are many successful businesses today which were started centuries ago without a business plan (this doesn't mean they didn't write a business plan at some point in the business). Most retail chains including Walmart (starting as a Nickel &Dime Store), eateries, bakeries, fuel stations, clothing companies, barbershops chains etc. started making their first sales without a business plan.

It will amaze you to know the number of well-documented business plans with colossal budgets which are parading the corridors of banks, investors and venture capitalists in search for funding. There are many more of these business plans under cupboards, in briefcases and drawers of 'wannapreneurs' which may never see the light of day.

If you are one of the entrepreneurs today who do not want to start a business with a written business plan, you are not alone. The real worth of your enterprise is in your operations not in your written plan.

WHY A <u>WRITTEN</u> BUSINESS PLAN IS NOT A MAJOR REQUIREMENT FOR STARTING A BUSINESS:

1. You can't tell what to expect.

As an entrepreneur who has identified a particular business niche, you cannot risk committing too much money or wasting too much time to start your operations. Your business should be fluid enough for you to start with the least you have, learn and understand the market before you can effectively structure the business operations in response to your market.

Sitting down to study the tides will never get a sailor to set sail. In every business is a hidden treasure which you have to venture to be able to capture. The word *venture* is one of the foremost words synonymously used for business. Your venture cannot sit in the cupboard as a written piece. Your venture is on the ground for you to capture. A savvy entrepreneur can always start a business venture without having any need for a written business plan.

2. Pick a venture you have some experience in.

Having insight in a particular business will win you more favour from the *spirits* of success (if there are any) than doing the reverse. Out of experience or insight comes the confidence to stay put in the uncertain tides of starting and running a small business. The stress associated with starting a business from the scratch is real and a business plan could be easily thrown off gear. Venturing into a business in which you have enough insight or have some first-hand experience in would guarantee your success. With enough insight and experience, you can say to a ten-page business plan idea, "Screw it!"

3. Carry out reality checks and make appropriate plans.

A business plan can comfortably exist in the minds of any serious and savvy entrepreneur. You don't need to read the encyclopaedia to inform you that, you need to make appropriate checks and cognitive analysis of your choice of business and the best location for such a business, before putting your money and effort into it.

With such key insight at hand, a reality check could be done on a week by week basis to understand your cash flow pattern in relation to the business environment you operate in. With this, you can make quarterly and yearly projections and also determine the areas of your business which need more focus in terms of investment.

4. The real test of your business is in the doing.

People place too much emphasis on a business plan than learning how to start it. There are some people whose only business experience is writing business plans. So they have about 20 business plans in their emails searching for funding. The real test of any business is in the doing. You have to get past the rhetoric and get to work. You will make mistakes, yes! But mind you, they will make you smart.

If you start small, you can quickly learn from your mistakes and improve. Soon you will be a very savvy entrepreneur who runs a multinational business.

Don't listen to the fear mongers who do not want to take a sip but relish getting drunk. Get to work! Start with what you have.

5. Build momentum for progress.

One of the most frustrating things about starting a business is looking at the journey to the top from the bottom. Most small business owners cannot wait to be in their BMWs and showing of their millionaire status. You have to know that, the man at the top did not fall there. You have to work your way to the top.

People do not know that preparation to succeed is an integral part of success. They lose sight of the years of hard work and sacrifice which successful entrepreneurs had to endure in order to merit their stay at the top.

You need to build momentum for progress. Don't be worried about who is going to finance your business venture from the start. Start small and build momentum.

Start in your dorm room, in your briefcase, on your smartphone or in the small corner of your room. Don't be stressed by the pressure of writing a 10-page business plan which will end up under your bed and may even bar you from making your first sale. Now look at point 5 above and read it again! Yes. That's what you need to do now. Dump the business plan idea!

6. Be open to new opportunities.

A business plan provides a kind of straightjacket for your business to operate in. The opportunities available to you when you wrote your business plan may have changed by the time you want to make use of them. Be open to new opportunities. Look out for the taste and preferences of your customers. Look at the trends and make out the changes that can work in your favour.

Monitor your business as it grows and align it to the key areas that have more prospects for steady positive cash flow.

You will be amazed how fast you can grow if you set your business antennas wide to scout for the opportunities in your field.

7. You need social capital, not a business plan.

No business plan is as good as goodwill. Be truthful to yourself, your staff and your customers. Be frank with your suppliers and creditors. Be useful to your community and let your business lend a hand to the less privileged.

The amount of social capital you will gain can take you farther than the money any profit-motivated investor can give you.

Once you understand what you are doing, social capital will take you farther than your business plan!

#6: SOURCES OF FUNDING

There is an adage in Akan which reads, *"Nipa wɔ nsusuyɛ, na aka sika."* This is literary translated as, "Humans have a lot of plans, but what is left is money to accomplish them." If there is anything that holds back success, it will be this statement.

You do not need money to execute your plans. Money cannot hold back your business plans. There are more than one sources of funding to kick start your small business. You have to open your mind up to new possibilities.

TOP 3 QUESTIONS ON FINANCING ANY BUSINESS

1. How much do you need?

You say you need money to start a business, right? Alright! So, if you meet an angel investor who is ready to finance your business today, can you state emphatically how much you need? No 'guesstimates' here!

Most people conceal their laziness and ineptitude behind the cloak of lack of money to start a business. When confronted by a potential to make their dreams come true, they soon realise that what they needed was not even money. Money is the least of the basic requirements to start a business.

Ask yourself now. How much in actual terms do you need to start your business? I mean an actual budget of how much you need to start your business, indicating the areas and how much in percentage terms you are going to spend within a specific period to meet your desired target?

Now you know that you do not need money to start a business. Money is probably the last thing you need now. You need a budget which states in no uncertain terms how much you need and how you intend to spend it.

Now get to work!

2. How soon do you need it? Or when do you need it?

Many people come to me to seek business advice.

They mostly do not leave without talking about their lack of money.

The question most fail to answer correctly has always been, how soon they need the money? Apparently, their answer at all times has been, "now"!

I have come to know that it is people with a dire financial situation who go cap in hand looking for money to start a business. To succeed in getting the money now than later, one should prove that they do not need the money.

In reverse, the money needs them. The world is replete with people who want to put money where it can grow. People who have and are able to multiply money, would not sink a USD $1,000 in a pit, just because a mentee or close business associate claims he or she has some knowledge of starting a certain business.

The truth I have learnt over the years is that people who come cap in hand, mostly need money for their bellies – not their businesses.

Nonetheless, you may need money later on a specific date – say 2nd June 2020, to start your business.

As I am writing this book today, I know when this book will be published and how much I would need to do so. The time span between now and when the book is published, is the time ABN Communications, my publishing company will strategize to promote and raise the needed resources to actualize the dream. This involves a well-rehearsed strategy on financing, production, promotion, marketing and sales.

There is a winning financial equation I would like to share with you.

Business Plan (BP) without Financial Plan (FP) is just a wish (WH).

Therefore: $BP - FP = WH$

In addition, Financial Plan (FP) without a Business Plan (BP) is a wind (WD).

Thus: $FP - BP = WD$

Every business plan needs to go hand in hand with a financial plan for one to attain the lifeblood of business which is Money or Financial Success (FS).

Meaning: $BP + FP = FS$

A business plan without a financial plan is just a *wish* - everyone has one.

A financial plan without a business plan is a *wind*. The wind has many directions and can disappear in no time. A business plan should always move with a financial plan for you to achieve financial success.

The main reason why people sit down for years without starting a business is that they do not have money to start. Thus, they have a business plan but no financial plan. If you are in this category, you could have started last year with a financial plan of raising GHC 1,000.

You would have been able to start your business in January this year if you had made plans for it a year (s) before. Doing it later will make it greater.

Proper financial projections often give you the opportunity to strategize and as well raise capital for business.

3) What are your sources of finance?

a. Personal Savings & Assets

When I was in Senior High School (SHS), I developed a good savings habit as at that time. I managed to save a little bit of my lunch money and over the three year SHS period, I had accrued GHC 100. This was accrued from monies I carefully saved and invested in a mutual fund, over the 3 year period in school. I was an excited young member of the savings and investment club, Young Investors Club back then in Senior High School, Prempeh College.

This notwithstanding, my financial literacy was limited to savings and investments. I didn't have any profound insight in money matters. I had a financial plan but to what end? I didn't have a business plan to complement my financial plan. So the obvious happened.

After school the whirlwinds of childish longings, made me spend my hard earned GHC 100 on game consoles. After all, as a teenager, I needed to refresh myself and not have a boring pre-university homestay.

As bad as my money habits were at that time, so many people are not out of the woods yet. Their preoccupation is to have a new shirt, shoe and handbag - a new this and a new that. All their savings go into buying these things (stuff). Meanwhile, they are the first to talk about lack of capital for business when the subject of entrepreneurship is mentioned.

You can start with what you have in your hand. This is your asset. Write a budget stating exactly how much you need over a certain period of time and work towards it.

In business, you need to have more skin in the game to stay in the game. So give yourself a heads up. Give up the frivolous expenditures. Start with what you have and others will meet you halfway.

b. Family & Friends

Family and friends present the most helpful source of funding for small businesses. Family and friends would not want to see you fail. You may be lucky to get your first start-up capital from a friend or family member. It is also easy for you to raise small loans from a family member or friend than from a total stranger. Such people will not demand any business plan to justify the viability of your small business idea. They will also not request for collateral as banks do. Neither are they mostly interested in equity (a percentage stake in your business) as requested for by venture capitalist and investors.

This notwithstanding, an individual looking for financial support from either friends or family members should clarify their motives of giving. It should be made clear that such gifts are only an expression of a kind gesture and will later not find its way in the loan books of the giver.

Loans from friends, thus friendly loans should always be taken with appropriate documentation, witnesses and well elaborate terms of repayment. This loan may bounce back later in your business life as an albatross around your neck if it is not taken under verifiable circumstances.

I have witnessed a situation where an interest-free loan of USD $1,000 for 5 years from a friend of a small business owner, metamorphosed into a debt payable with 10%

interest over the same period of time. This happened when the creditor was shocked to see the success of his friend's business over the said period of time.

Don't let this happen to you.

c. Investors

Investors form a core group for sourcing business finance. They may come across as either active or passive investors. Active investors or shareholders invest their money in a business venture, engage in the day to day management of the business as members of the Board of Directors and influence the day to day management of the business.

Passive investors are also simply referred to as *equity holders*. They leave the day to day running of the business to the CEO and his/her team and hold them accountable for a return on their investment. Unlike active investors, passive investors do sell their stake in the business whenever they deem fit. Investors bring in extra capital and expertise but also call for strict accountability. Shareholders share the risk as well as demand a good return on their investment.

d.   Retained profits

Retained profit is monies retained in a business accruing from profits made over a period. A savvy businessman knows what to purchase with his business profits in other to make more profits.

Warren Buffet started making money from one pinball machine which he put in a barbershop in Washington DC, USA. When he made enough profit, USD $25 at the time, he purchased another pinball machine which he put in another barbershop.

Over time, he had pinball machines in many locations across the city. Though his pinball machine business was sold after his first year of operations for over USD $ 1,000, young Warren managed to raise enough capital of over USD $5,000 now equivalent to USD $53,000 from his pinball machine business at the age of 17 years to set up more profitable businesses – a precursor to his billionaire status today.

Reinvesting retained profits, thus recapitalization of your business for growth will not cost your business any extra cash which could be lost in high-interest rates if your business rather went for a loan from the bank. This is a prudent way of using your own financial resource for business.

e. Bank loans

Bank loans are a rich source of funding given the roles that banks play in major economies. Small businesses may take loans from financial institutions to support their day to day operations.

Similarly, banks provide credit facilities to businesses as working capital as well as mortgages for non-current assets such as land and buildings.

One way you can build good creditworthiness with a bank as a small business is to open a corporate account for your business, one which attracts excellent interest rate. As you continue to deposit and withdraw money from your bank, your statement of account could serve as a guarantee for your loan repayment.

It should be well noted that loans are not gratuitous. You, therefore, need to check the terms of repayment and the interest rate payable before you take any loan from a financial institution.

f. Government Grant/Loans

It is said that it is not the business of government to be in business. The major stakeholders in the creation of jobs are the financial players (banks) and the private sector.

In order to stimulate the growth of business and create the enabling environment for businesses to thrive, the government often comes out with loans and grants to help the players in the private sector and sometimes provide liquidity support for banks through the central or federal bank. Whereas grants are free-targeted funds for businesses, government loans attract an interest rate which is often below the going market rate.

Whichever way you see government loans, they are not for free. It requires the same measure of caution needed when taking a loan from the various financial institutions.

g. Business Angels

Business angels are a remarkable source of start-up funding. Angels are shrewd businessmen and women who examine the viability of a business idea having studied the business plan under their magnifying lenses.

A business angel who is convinced about the viability of a said business would go ahead and dole out money for the setting up or expansion of same. Besides financial assistance, angels get out of their way to open up young business owners to their contacts, wide business connections and network to provide sufficient resource for the growth of their businesses. Business angels often do this in exchange for an equity stake in the businesses they support. Some do it out of sheer benevolence.

h. Venture Capital

Another word which is usually used for venture capital is 'private equity'. This is a type of investment that embodies funds managed by professional investors. Venture capitalists hardly put their monies in start-ups or small businesses. They usually invest in high performing businesses with good fundamentals. They prefer to invest in businesses which have already established themselves.

As an exit strategy or an early retirement plan, founders of most successful companies sell a majority stake in their businesses to venture capitalists in exchange for cash or bonds.

i) Crowdfunding

Crowdfunding according to Wikipedia is *the practice of funding a project or venture by raising small amounts of money from a large number of people, typically via the internet.* Crowdfunding works best for non-profit projects including those of social enterprises and NGOs.

Are you an entrepreneur? Your project can raise millions on crowdfunding platforms such as Indiegogo, Kickstarter, Gofundme, Fundable, etc.

To succeed on crowdfunding sites, you need to learn how to craft heart touching stories, thus, knowing how to *put the begging on.* It will be worthwhile to improve your internet savviness and your ability to reach a large number of potential donors through social media.

Since its debut in 2010, GoFundMe, the biggest crowdfunding platform has raised over USD $ 5 billion dollars. Today, the site receives over $140 million in donations per month. It is a platform worth exploring!

UNIT 13

HOW TO START SMALL

Business Name

● ● ● ● ●

What is in a business name?

Unless a successful rebranding is done over time that which we call a particular business name, by any other name would lose its value totally.

I.K Adusei

─────────────────────────────────

What is in a name? This is an old aged question.

William Shakespeare tried to rally the minds of thinkers around the significance of names given to objects, persons and entities. In his world-famous book Romeo and Juliet, William Shakespeare wrote these lines:

"Tis but thy name that is
mine enemy:
What's Montague? It is not
hand nor foot,
Nor arm, nor face, nor any
other part.
What's in a name? That which we call a rose,
By any other name would
smell as sweet."

In this piece, Juliet argued that there was nothing extraordinary in the name Montague – being that, the family of Montague had an unsympathetic rivalry with Juliet's family. Juliet fell in love with Romeo who was from the rival family of Montague. In an attempt to justify her love for Romeo, she claimed that if Romeo had been called by any other name, he would still be as sweet and thereby her lover.

Can this assertion be justified in business? If Coca-Cola was called Jilt, would Jilt taste as sweet? Would Jilt still remain the number two beverage company in the world? What about if Coca-Cola changes its name three times in a year, from Coca-Cola to Jilt, Bronze and Kite. Would the brand still be trusted and valuable?

With all severity, Juliet's accession flies sharply in the face of conventional business practice. The argument can only retain its validity in the relationship realm as a *romance message*. In the realm of business, a name has everything extraordinary associated with it. The choice of business name has psychological, legal and fiscal ramifications on any business.

Dangote Cement cannot be swapped with Nestlé Ideal Milk for the milk to taste as good. Neither can Coca-Cola brand change its name to Peace Cola and still remain as valuable.

What is in a business name?

Unless a successful rebranding is done over time that which we call a particular business name, by any other name would lose its value totally.

3 MAJOR WAYS YOUR CHOICE OF BUSINESS NAME AFFECTS YOUR BUSINESS

1. If your business is easy to pronounce, people will favour you more.

In 2014, I came across a bank which was then called, First Capital Plus Bank. My first impression was that the name of the bank was too long for me to consider opening an account with them.

It was too difficult for me to pronounce the name of the bank without forgetting a word or two from the name. I may be very dumb to encounter such difficulty but there may be many dumb people like me whose money the bank may be looking for.

Somewhere in 2016, there were huge billboards in the streets of Accra and numerous LPMs (Live Presenter Mentions) on radio and TV which announced the change of name of the bank from First Capital Plus Bank to Capital Bank.

I wasn't surprised at all about the new development but the sad thing was that the bank had been in the dark (unattractive) for far too long.

Fast forward 2018, there was news of liquidity (money) challenges hitting the newly branded bank leading to its imminent collapse the same year.

There may be a lot of factors which could have contributed to the demise of the bank but from the onset, it was clear that such an unattractive name was enough testament to result in low patronage hence their lack of money to run their operations.

It should be noted that sales also referred to as money, is the lifeblood of any business. Always bear in mind that, if your business is easy to pronounce, people (sales) will favour you more.

2. The simpler the better.

In an attempt not to limit the ill fate of Capital Bank to its initial long name, First Capital Plus Bank, Capital Bank could have been the best choice of name to start with. In business, you need to know how to use the Keep It Simple and Sexy (*KISS*) tactic. It is a rich ingredient in any sales and marketing meal. The simpler the name the better. Always *keep it simple and sexy (KISS)*.

3. Checking Availability of Names

One major thing that may affect your business from the onset, is the lack of due diligence.

In the books of the registrar of companies in any country are names of companies which may either be functioning or locked up in briefcases and cupboards. Whether a business is functioning or not, you need to be sure of the availability of the name (whether or not it is registered) in the books of the registrar general.

Many entrepreneurs fail to follow such simple but priceless business advice, only to realise later that a certain company has already registered their business name.

In this case, the only remedy is a change of business name which may require financial obligations owing to change of logos, letterheads, flyers, sign boards, banners and other ad tools.

The greatest loss would have to do with the challenge of communicating such a blander to your many customers and its accompanying effect on the image of your brand.

Simple due diligence of checking the availability of names in the records of appropriate authorities can save your business from needless financial loss.

FREQUENTLY ASKED QUESTIONS (FAQ)

In the many events, training programs, conferences and workshops hosted by my non – profit business Africa Business Network (ABN), I have had the rare privilege of being confronted by participants with mixed questions on starting and running a business. Here is a cross-section of some of the major questions which may be of some use to you.

1. Q: *I want to set up a team for my business. What are the basic things you would look out for when hiring your staff?*

IK: It is good to hire people who demonstrate commitment and dedication to work. But over the years I have come to learn that, to hire a committed and devoted person who is not trustworthy is a launch pad for failure in business. Trustworthiness stands out among all the basic things to look out for when hiring.

Unfortunately, no one comes to a job interview with trustworthiness boldly inscribed on their foreheads. So you have to hire the most disciplined people and monitor them closely to identify the traits of commitment, dedication and above all trustworthiness. Keep those who have the latter.

As an employer, the buck stops with you. You remain fully responsible for the team you choose to work with. So you need to put in place a robust system to check the conducts of your employees – even those you deem trustworthy.

2. Q: *Why do you think it is important to think big?*

IK: It doesn't cost a *pesewa* to think big. It is absolutely free. It takes the same energy to think big as to think small. True success always has a small beginning. To ever succeed you need to think big. It cost USD $ 0.00 to think like a billionaire. This is why it is important to think big! After all, if you succeed you win; if you don't, you lose nothing.

3. Q: *I have about USD $ 10,000 to invest in a business. Which business do you think will give me a good return on my investment?*

IK: Like real estate, location is key to business success. While a business will do well in a certain location, it will perform poorly in another.

Carefully study the needs of your immediate community. Find a need that is related to your passion or interest and make sure people will be ready to pay for your product or service. Such a business should be scalable for you to achieve maximum financial rewards.

Design a creative way to make money by selling a product or service. With the best business practices and principles – most of which are encased in this book, you will guarantee yourself a good return on your USD $ 10,000 investment.

4. Q: *What keeps you going when the going gets tough?*

IK: I have a plaque on my desk that reads:

BUSINESS IS ABOUT BUILDING THE FUTURE. DON'T LET TODAY'S CHALLENGES HOLD YOU BACK. – I.K Adusei

This keeps me going no matter what.

5. Q: *I believe in financial literacy. Do you think financial literacy should be made a core subject in our schools?*

IK: This is a very good question. My answer is an absolute yes! Financial literacy should be thought in schools from first grade to the tertiary level. This is the only way we can create an enabling environment for private sector growth in any economy.

When people are financially literate, they can create surpluses (savings and investments) which the banks can use to support their liquidity situation. They can give out more loans to support businesses.

More financial surplus means more seed capital available for the creation of more businesses. ABN through its flagship program *Commence* is working hard to make this possible. Check our website now www.abnonline .org and search for ABN Unite for more updates!

6. Q: *I have a small business. I always find out that my workers steal from me. What can I do now since I do not have money to invest in high tech security systems?*

IK: Walmart started as a Nickel and Dime Store in Arkansas, USA with no sophisticated security systems. Today it is the largest department store in the world.

If you don't have high tech security systems keep your eyes and ears wide open and be your own security until you can afford one. Keep as little cash as possible at your workplace. Keep only what your business would need for the day to day operations. Any excess cash should be kept in your corporate bank account. This will save you from the shock of losing all your business capital after you have entrusted all your money in the care of your subordinates (ie. your accountant, cashier, shop attendant or managers).

Employ a good accounting system which will help you keep track of your daily records to minimize or regulate theft. Big banks with high tech security systems have theft issues among their staff. So, be vigilant! If you sleep after your investments, you will always have nightmares.

7. Q: *I am a Senior High School graduate. My parents have no money for my tertiary education. I want to set up a business to repair tech gadgets and build computer software. What can I do now?*

IK: It is good to identify your passion and interest. However, you need to be on top of your game in order to get anywhere. In whatever you do, aim at being the best.

For now, you need the skills and know-how to be able to ply your trade. In your case, you can apply to be an apprentice or intern with a firm or business which repairs tech gadgets. Whilst there, I am sure you will find people who can teach you Computer Programming. Such people may be customers of the company or some of your colleagues at work. Take the opportunity to learn all you can - both on your own and on the job. Plus, there is a lot of information on entrepreneurship skills development available on the home page of ABN's website. With strong determination and the pursuit of purpose, you will succeed!

8. Q: *If you were 24 years today and were offered a USD $ 100.00 to start a business, which business would you start?*

IK: At age 24 without enough financial or business skills, it would be easy to waste your resources on unprofitable ventures. USD $100.00 will be too small today to turn your fortunes around within a short period of time.

However, for any business to be most profitable it should be scalable, thus able to grow, multiply and become replicable in different locations.

In my location, I would start a French home tuition program with no money at all. As a polyglot, word of mouth advertisement will help me get my first client. I will later rent a venue (classroom) when I get enough cash from my first client. With this, I can scale up the business as I recruit other teachers who can take care of the various classes.

9. Q: *My name is Kobby. I just completed University of Ghana with a Degree in Political Science. I have leadership skills. Which business would be most suitable for me?*

IK: Leadership skills are central to all endeavours of life including business. You need to identify your particular skills which you can sell to make money. It could be writing, swimming or cooking. It could also be sales or marketing skills, IT skills or fitness training skills. Structure a business around your key skills to be able to make a profit. Soon you will be successful!

10. Q: *I have read your book From Nowhere to Somewhere. I have been able to identify my purpose for*

life. I want to be a best seller someday. How do I succeed in publishing?

IK: The best way to be a good writer is to be an avid reader. Be ready to read other peoples' materials and soon people will read your materials.

Find an area you are comfortable with. Start writing articles and soon you will be writing a book.

If you have a business plan, you need a financial plan to achieve success. Set timelines and get to work. A business plan without a financial plan is just a wish.

EPILOGUE

"To build a successful business, you must start small and dream big."

– Aliko Dangote

To be able to start a business and create wealth you need to do things in a certain way. You need to arm yourself with the principles used by successful global entrepreneurs. It is by doing things in a certain way that you attain the true wealth that abound in the world of entrepreneurship. There are seven must dos for would-be successful entrepreneurs. By far, all globally successful entrepreneurs who started small still have the same routine every day of their lives.

Seven Must Dos:

Daily Routines of Successful Entrepreneurs

1. Get Good Financial Education: Money is all around you

In Wallace D. Wattles' book *The Science of Getting Rich*, he dismissed the lifelong contention that life is a competition for resources in which the fittest survive. According to him, there are infinite resources available to everyone. The competition for scarce resources is, therefore, a needless undertaking.

Money is all around us. Resources are never scarce and more resources can be created out of nothing if we look beyond our scarcity mentality.

The guy that constantly asked for directions helped google to invent Google Maps. The woman who was late to work and asked a friend for a lift helped create the ride sharing app Lyft. The man who asked for a spare room in his friend's vacation home abroad helped birth Airbnb services.

Money is all around us. Those who look beyond scarcity usher themselves into a world of limitless possibilities.

Your ability to see money, where others see problems will largely hinge on the extent of the financial education you have. The depth of your financial education will depend on your level of financial literacy and your understanding of how to generate positive cash flow in your bid to start small and grow big in business.

To master these areas in business you would need to read this book over again. People with little or no financial education end up with a mountain of debt and limited financial possibilities. *How to Start Small* is replete with information on financial success. It was written to help you unlock the doors to your financial freedom. Have a real communion with this book. Get a good financial education while you can.

2. The Golden Rule: Pay yourself first

To be able to start small and keep your business running effectively, you need to know and understand the golden rule of business.

With golden rules, those who have the gold make the rules.

Pay yourself first! This is the golden rule for financial freedom.

The size of your wealth is not dependent on how much money you make but how much you keep and invest.

If you have a monthly salary of GHC 1,000 and spend GHC 1,300 each month you are not financially wealthy. You are in financial distress.

The golden rule of wealth creation is to create excess money through prudent spending, saving and investment.

Pay yourself first out of every money you make! A part of every money you make is yours to keep – save and invest to provide capital or funding for the success of your own business.

Don't give all your income, take-home pay or pocket money to your mobile operator, dressmaker, tax collector, utility service owner, owners of supermarket and grocery stores, etc.

Every *cedi* you spend on your daily needs makes the provider of such goods and services richer. Even though you may not have enough, you will always have money (even if borrowed) to make your mobile operator, dressmaker, tax collector, utility service owner, owners of supermarket and grocery stores, etc. richer anytime you request for their services.

Gold cometh gladly and in increasing quantity to any man who will put by not less than one-tenth of his earnings to create an estate for his future and that of his family.

– George S. Clason

By paying yourself first, thus putting not less than one-tenth of your earnings aside as an investment for your future, before you pay any other person, you give yourself a chance to be rich too.

Contribute to your own success. Always remember the golden rule: Pay yourself first! It is apparent that those who have the gold will continue to make the rules.

3. The Power of Self – Sacrifice: Control your expenditure

Entrepreneurship is a lonely journey which requires a lot of self-sacrifices. To start small, grow big and stay on top, self-sacrifice is a basic requirement. Human needs are infinite. The more money you make the greater your purchasing power. It is what you spend your money on that makes you rich or poor.

Self - sacrifice is the ability to keep your expenditure low to create surplus, even when your income or earnings increase.

According to Robert T. Kiyosaki, the main reason why the rich keep getting richer, the poor getting poorer and the middle-class keep shrinking is that the rich buy their luxuries last while the poor and middle-class buy their luxuries first.

The rich are able to endure long years of financial discipline, denying themselves of things which the poor and middle-class spend their money on in order to create a surplus to be reinvested in other business ventures.

The poor struggle to make money but their lack of financial discipline makes them poor. They spend ALMOST ALL their money on goods and services provided and supplied by rich merchants.

The middle-class always look rich. Their lifestyle of keeping up with the Joneses keeps them always in debt – spending money they do not even have.

To create wealth, you need to create a surplus. To create a surplus, you need to control your expenditure. To attain true financial freedom, one needs to defer his or her current gratification for future financial freedom. Control your expenditure now to become financially wealthy!

4. Protect Your Purse: Don't lend, give

After controlling your expenditure and having a surplus to invest in your business, you need to protect your purse.

A part of being real with others, is being true to yourself. One of the most terrible ways to lose your investment is through lending. I have come across a lot of people who lament on their debtors' inability to repay their debt. This poor financial habit predisposes most people to lose more money than financial institutions.

After painful years of self-sacrifice and financial restraints, most people give away their monies to close friends and family relations who come to them for loans. These borrowers do not care to know the number of months or years you took to raise the money for which they so desperately crave. These types of loans are usually misused and end up becoming a bad debt.

To save your start-up capital from been misused by cronies and relatives who can't save a penny, don't lend but give! Give the least you can to help others get through their problems. In other words, lend what you can comfortably lose.

If someone comes to borrow GHC 800 out of your GHC 1000 savings, you can give the fellow GHC 50 for free with no strings attached. In this case, the borrower won't curse you for giving him/her GHC 50 for free.

You would have saved yourself the headache of losing GHC 800 to a good friend who the misfortunes of financial distress has fallen on. You will save yourself from the acrimony which would ensue if such a person is unable to repay the loan of GHC 800.

Similarly, you will save your dream of starting your own business from dying an unnatural death. Be smart with your finances. Don't lend, give!

5. Self – Development: Money chases a distinct few

Unemployment numbers are staggering everywhere in the world.

This notwithstanding, money continues to chase a distinct few. No matter how bad the economy of your country is, there are people making good returns on their investment. The gap between the haves and have nots is widening. The solution to this sorry situation is *self-development.*

How prepared are you for the opportunity you are looking for?

What is your depth of understanding in the business you want to venture into?

Are you on top of the numbers in your current business?

Books, seminars, workshops, travel etc. are key components of self-development. How much cash have you spent on your self-development this year?

The grass is always greener where skills are honed and talents sharpened. The key is for you to develop yourself. Money is all around you.

6. Be ready for the Nos: Have pure tenacity of purpose

The closer you are to reaching your goal, the louder the voices of the naysayers. No matter the number of NOs you hear, you need to keep moving forward. Your dreams should be anchored by pure tenacity of purpose.

Somewhere in China, in the year 1999, years before he came into the limelight, Jack Ma, Founder of Alibaba repeated this statement to his Alibaba team:

Today is hard, tomorrow will be worse but the day after tomorrow will be sunshine.

To start small and grow big, tenacity of purpose is paramount.

7. Start Small Unnoticed: Success is a day by day journey

As an entrepreneur, you owe yourself all the answers to your business questions. Many are those who would want to see faster results from processes they have no idea about.

In most situations, many entrepreneurs are caught in the web of trying to prove critics wrong. They end up focusing too much on the public outlook of the business than the actual work at hand.

To succeed in business, you need to start small unnoticed. Make all the mistakes there is to make and learn as much as you can. As you learn to oil your lump, the media will be on the lookout for you. By that time, you would have a lot under your belt.

Always remember, the key is to start small unnoticed, success is a day by day journey.